Good Dog Behaviour
By Choice
Through Positive Canine Coaching

And

Enrichment Through Scentwork
for Highly Aroused Dogs

Sally Gutteridge

Copyright

Interior Layout: Sandeep Likhar

Books may be purchased by contacting the publisher and author at:
info@sallygutteridge.com
www.sallygutteridge.com

Imprint: Independently published
© 2018 by Sally Gutteridge.

Welcome to Mission Possible Solutions.

These books are a series of dog guides designed to make positive canine coaching accessible and understandable. This edition contains the first and second guides in the series. I have tried to keep as close to the original guides as possible but minimise repeated instructions and suggest you work through them with your dog as two separate books.

Each guide covers a single source topic with natural progression through ten carefully created easy-to-follow missions. Whilst small, Mission Possible books pack a big punch as they are concise and provide a huge amount of value to readers and their dogs. If you dive into the tasks, you're going to have some great fun with your dog.

Most of all, Mission Possible books are interactive, positive, and build great dog skills. Each book contains bespoke professional guidance to learn specific skills for exceptional results.

About the Author

Sally Gutteridge has been a full-time educational writer since 2015 holding a variety of canine certifications. She is a former professional Dog Trainer with the Royal Army Veterinary Corps, former instructor with Hearing Dogs for Deaf People and has much rescue experience. Sally is a member of the Pet Professional Guild. She is a Graduate and award winner from The Writers Bureau. Through the organisation Canine Principles, Sally along with a fantastic team, provides reputable Continuation of Professional Development for all canine professionals. Canine Principles teaches the most up to date, positive, scientific canine awareness.

Sally lives in Rural Cumbria with her ever-patient husband and four rescued, cheeky terriers.

Table of Contents

Good Dog Behaviour
by Choice through Positive Canine
Coaching

Introduction

Welcome! The aim of this guide is to help you understand your dog and carry out positive canine coaching for a number of important tasks.

Dogs, at any given time, generally behave in a way that's natural to them — they don't automatically become easily managed, well-mannered and compliant just because we like that. They don't pop into the world with an ability to sit on cue and a heel position burned readily into their mind. Just like we learned to talk, walk and brush our teeth, dogs need to learn what things mean, before they can respond with the right choice. But even so, we see people saying sit and heel to dogs that have never been taught what it means over and over again. To dogs, they might as well just be saying 'bananas' for all the sense it makes.

There's good news though. With a few careful steps, some fundamental knowledge and a growing skill, you can become your dog's teacher, his coach. There's a whole science to coaching dogs based on how they learn and feel. This guide will teach you the science of canine coaching in a way that it seeps into your mind and puts down roots, all the while you are having fun with your dog.

The missions we teach here are not traditional obedience commands. We are not aiming for a robotic dog that can parade through a series of positions. We are going for ten cues that embrace your relationship whilst empowering both of you — and making you feel great.

If you feel up to it, you can document your progress through each mission with notes and pictures. To read your success story would truly make my day, so feel free to post it on my Facebook page at https://www.facebook.com/sallyanddogs/ visit my website at sallygutteridge.com or email me at info@sallygutteridge.com. I always respond to every message.

Note: I refer to dogs in the book as "him" purely for ease of reading; the advice applies to males and females in equal measure.

Part One:
Coach How Dogs Learn

Dogs are amazing, communicative, loyal and dependable companions. They don't ask for much and don't complain much either. Whilst they are thought to have crept into our lives as wolf-like ancestor thousands of years ago, there is no animal today that remotely compares.

However, dogs are still fairly misunderstood. Even though in the 21st century we know so much about them, people still mistreat dogs. Perpetuated by the media and despite evidence to the contrary, dogs are still abused or inadequately taken care of by many people, including dog professionals.

A vast number of learned professionals and even scientists are exploring the intricate details of dog domestication. One day, there will no longer be people telling confused dog guardians to be the boss or practice dominance and dogs will get the true understanding they fully deserve. While I don't want to dwell on the bad stuff for long, I must share the reason why we don't need to be the boss and where that idea came from in the first place.

The History

There was a study on a group of unrelated wolves, carried out to find out how they behave when observed. They were not a family and they didn't get on very well. The conclusion was drawn after a few months that the tension was based on every animal being keen to lead the group. It's unclear why that conclusion was drawn, but it was quickly also applied to domestic dogs.

A few years after this theory was presented, another study took place, this time by a different scientist who recognized the flaws of the first, which were plentiful.

Natural, wild wolves live in family groups, and all members of the pack are somehow related, so studying unrelated wolves is more of a wolf social experiment than reality. Studying captive unrelated wolves is as natural as assuming people live like they are all on Big Brother, and we know how fraught with tension and squabbles that is.

The family group consists of the breeding parents and their offspring. They live together, hunt together, play and eat as a family. Parents guide with kindness and cubs defer with respect. There are few physical reprimands and aggression is rare, much like any good, loving family group. Wolves successfully communicate with a slightly different ear position, a glance, a brief posture or facial expression. It's amazing to see.

Meanwhile, dog trainers that still embrace the idea that wolves have a power quest and that dogs are inherently wolves, decided that being the alpha wolf to their dog was of high importance. In fact, some believed that if they establish themselves as the Alpha wolf, all the dog's problems would naturally melt away. So, people everywhere started going through doors first, eating from their dog's bowl and standing in their beds. I imagine their dogs were somewhat perplexed, as patient as they may be though.

The Consequence

When this weirdness didn't solve problems such as lead pulling or jumping on the furniture, dog trainers hung onto the theory regardless, as many people do. There's social safety in sticking to our beliefs along with a generous dash of ego. Trainers started to become forceful, to establish their place as the alpha wolf (it sounds ridiculous because it is). This is where force and fear-based dog training originated — if the dog didn't respond to being second through a door by not pulling on the lead, he was considered dominant and forced into submission. According to this idea, dominant dogs were everywhere, planning to take over the world!

Next, we saw painful collars, alpha rolls and general physical punishment. Dogs suffered for human ignorance and many still do. Humanity is slow at keeping up with new developments. We make our mind up on something based on our first experience of it, then gather evidence to reinforce our set belief – often for the rest of our lives. Even today, long after the original theory was revoked, there are still far too many 'pack leaders' stalking the dog world, giving the worst possible advice, ignoring the truth and yet selling their services as dog professionals.

The Biology

There's another reason that we can't possibly believe and use the alpha wolf theory. Even if wolves did live with tension and a quest to be the boss in every social group — which we have established they don't — dogs have thousands of years of evolution between them and their wild cousins.

Evolution of any species is based on successful reproduction. If the species don't reproduce in their current environment, they become extinct. However, dogs have been reproducing in domestication for thousands of years now, and have literally evolved to live alongside people with, and even carry out tasks for people. If DNA were an individual, it would be a genius, adapting to be a bit more suitable for the environment with any generation. Wolves living in the wild as a family are rightfully scared of people due to mass persecution. Dogs sitting on your sofa has thousands of years adapted DNA, to live in your home as a companion and friend. Your dog already knows he's not a wolf and knows you are not a wolf either. It doesn't take a genius to work that out and our dogs are pretty astute.

The Future

It's not all bad news and stubborn pack leaders though. There is a growing, evolving movement within the dog community that embraces ethology and science. Ethology is the study of animals in their natural environment, whereas science is generally either proven or the most likely theory on anything.

Science currently tells us that kind, motivational teaching has excellent results and ethology tells us that dogs are happiest with a positive, kind and force-free approach. Trainers that learned the old methods initially are changing over and embracing kindness, there is a new generation of dog professionals spreading the word that 'pack leadership' is a myth and causes problems. Highly educated ethologists are presenting new evidence all the time that dogs excel to be the best they can be, with positive treatment and teaching.

Canine Coaching

Canine coaching is kind. Based on empowerment of the dog, we change our perspective as a coach. We don't see behaviour as a thing to be changed, no matter what it takes, we see it as a symptom of a feeling and work out why that feeling may exist. The coach works with the dog's inner state, his freedom to make choices and his uniqueness. Coaching accepts and embraces the dog's rights to be free of force and fear.

Canine coaches work through their minds and hearts, to inspire the dog to find and use his natural strengths. The missions in this book will help you become a successful canine coach, and your dog will love you for it.

The Important Bits

There are some things you need to know about your dog. The fundamentals of teaching that apply to dogs, and interestingly to people too. So, let's explore the facts and theories which positive coaching is based on such as how your dog learns and how his brain works.

When your dog was born, learning began right away, well almost. After the first couple of weeks he began trying new things. If he liked the result, the puppy would try it again, because the result was rewarding. Early in his life the puppy's brain is not fully formed – in fact it's barely formed at all so this early learning puts decisions and choices into the brain as it forms, so these choices and experiences become strong and well-established. By the time the puppy reaches adulthood, his brain will be filled with ideas about which choices worked, his habits will be formed.

Positive Reinforcement

Learning doesn't stop at puppyhood though, every time a dog tries something new, no matter what his age, he is making a choice. That choice will lead to a consequence and if the dog likes the consequence, he will make the same choice again.

This is the basis of positive reinforcement. In the same way, if a dog chooses to do something for the first time and the consequence is not rewarding to them, it's not being reinforced, so it will probably not be the dog's first choice next time.

Positive reinforcement means that a favourable consequence is linked in the dog's mind to a choice they make, so the choice is made stronger. Within coaching we can manipulate consequences by providing the dog with reward, to make the dog's good choices stronger than the choices that are not so good.

Why does this work so well?

Positive reinforcement is one of four learning processes which also include force and punishment.

If you like the scientific terms, they are called quadrants and include the following. Examples are in brackets below the definition.

- Positive reinforcement; something good starting. For example, giving the dog a treat for a good choice. (Stopping pulling and creating a loose lead)
- Negative reinforcement; something bad stopping. For example, loosening a choke collar for a good choice. (Stopping pulling on the lead)
- Positive punishment; something bad starting. For example, giving the dog a smack for a bad choice.

(Jumping up)

- Negative punishment; something good stopping. For example, withdrawing attention from the dog for a bad choice

(Nipping hands)

Take note of the first two points above. You can probably see that both approaches give the same result, a loose lead. There is a big difference though. Positive reinforcement empowers the dog, whilst negative reinforcement disempowers him. Negative reinforcement relies on something the dog dislikes, being done to him, to work. We must ask why, when rewarding the right choice has the same positive result.

The Dopamine Effect

There's another reason that positive reinforcement works so well, the neurotransmitter Dopamine. Neurotransmitters are brain messengers that change the way your dog feels, and Dopamine is a feel-good chemical that's rocket fuel for learning.

This neurotransmitter is a big part of reason dogs (and people) repeat behaviours that provided a reward. When something good happens, we get a Dopamine high and that's the chemical reason that the dog repeats something for a reward. Linked with motivation and building memories, this neurotransmitter is the neurological basis of positive reinforcement.

Dopamine is triggered by good feelings, play, reward, positive interactions, food and general rewarding experiences.

The Cortisol Effect

Whilst Dopamine is rocket fuel for memory and learning, Cortisol has the opposite effect. This hormone is the body's alarm system and causes a fight or flight reaction to keep the dog safe.

An ancient hormone, cortisol acts alongside adrenaline when the dog experiences a threat, to help him fight or run away, essentially to survive. This hormone does the same thing in our own bodies; when you go weak at the knees because something has made you jump, it's because your survival system has been triggered by the release of cortisol. The fight or flight system is split a little further, your dog may try to run away, try to chase the scary thing away, go to battle, freeze and hope the threat doesn't see him or fool around. Fooling around might involve jumping up or mouthing hands and clothing. All of these tell us the dog is stressed. Stress hinders learning, digestion, immunity and memory, it's a huge hindrance to learning.

Cortisol is a response to stress and is triggered by force, fear, confrontation or environmental tension – for example, something the dog is scared of being in his immediate environment. When dog training isn't positive and uses punishment, or force, the dog will experience stress and can't learn to his potential.

Our aim is to dial up the dopamine, avoid cortisol, teach some useful cues and have fun, so let's get going.

Takeaway Points

- Dogs and wolves are - behaviourally - completely different animals based on separate evolution and the domestication of dogs.
- There is no such thing as an alpha dog.
- Scientific and kind dog training shows empathy and education. Punishment and force show lack of both.
- Cortisol prevents learning. It's triggered by force, fear and punishment and is directly related to stress.
- Dogs learn from trying new things and dependent on the consequence they may or may not repeat their behaviour.
- Positive reinforcement is rewarding a choice, so the dog repeats it.
- Canine coaching empowers the dog and the coach.
- Dopamine aids memory and motivation. It is triggered by feeling good and reward.

Part Two: Preparation

The first part of any canine coaching must always be building a trusting relationship based on communication and observation. We can live with dogs, love them with all our hearts and simply not understand them. With the risky quality of people giving advice on dog behaviour in the world, we can even get professional advice and still misunderstand our dogs, leading to confusion and even worse, broken trust.

You may fully understand your dog already. You might have been through tough times with your friend and share a mutual frustration based on lack of understanding. You might have a little gentle puppy who is keen and willing to learn or a rescue dog who was abandoned at adolescence because he was never taught any manners, therefore was unmanageable.

This is the point we start afresh. The beauty of science-based coaching is that if we follow the right steps they will work.

The more help your dog needs to learn, the more different tricks we can use, but the steps work I promise you this.

Know Your Dog

Knowing your dog means that you empathise with him and try to see the world from his point of view and not your projection of him. Projection is something we do naturally and way more than is particularly healthy. We look at a stranger and decide how they feel, when we disagree with someone and things get heated, we decide how they feel – often without any evidence or communication.

We can look at our dogs and decide that their fear is naughtiness, their stress is because they are feeling obnoxious or their confusion ignorance. Even whilst none of these are true, they certainly make us feel differently about the dog and his behaviour.

Take some time out and just chill with your dog. Stop acting and responding and start observing. Ethology is the act of observing an animal in their natural environment, with no interference from the watcher. Become your dog's ethologist and learn from him.

Your dog's behaviour is a direct indication of how he feels. So, if he looks relaxed, he will be feeling relaxed. If your dog looks excited, he will be feeling excited and if his body tenses up, he is likely to be feeling pretty tense. The way a dog feels is usually dependent on what the environment around him is like.

There is an exception to this. When a dog is ill or in pain it will naturally change their behaviour and the way they look. Any unusual behaviour should be assessed by your veterinarian, to check your dog's health and wellbeing. When a dog is feeling poorly or in pain, it's their right to see the vet.

The dog with a clean bill of health, that has a behaviour change will usually do so based on an environment change. So, if your dog is asleep and the doorbell goes, there's an obvious change, he might bark and run around. If your dog is scared of bangs and is relaxed, but a firework goes off in the distance, his behaviour will change, he may tremble and hide. The dog that is scared of children might hear a scream and become tense then bark in response – telling the screamer to stay well away.

Your task is to witness these overt behaviour changes and empathise with your dog. He doesn't know who is at the door, he may feel that the firework is a direct threat to his survival or it could really hurt his ears. Your dog may never have never had a good experience with animated and noisy children, so is scared of them and gets defensive. When we start to observe with empathy, we stop focussing on the awkward behaviour and we place focus on how the dog feels and his motivation behind that particular display. When we start to approach observation from this viewpoint, we are becoming enlightened observers, we are ethologists.

The basis of any behaviour change is how the dog feels. The way he feels is usually triggered by the environment and the reason he chooses that particular behaviour is because he has learned to choose it in similar situations in the past. So, when you observe your dog, ask yourself, how does my dog feel, what has made him feel that way and what is reinforcing this type of response.

Because a consequence will always drive behaviour, without fail, if your dog finds that his behaviour worked in a situation, that behaviour will get stronger by repetition. Here's a common example:

My terrier, Chips is socially awkward and somewhat fearful of other dogs. He actually really likes other dogs and with proper introduction he will be friendly and enjoy a brief hello. He's much more comfortable with the smaller dogs and those that don't have obscured faces, such as long haired or black dogs which are more difficult for others to read.

When he sees a dog that he's not comfortable with, Chips will put on an aggressive display – as Braveheart terriers often do when they feel awkward or worried. His display can easily become full on lunging and barking, whilst on the lead. The consequence from his 40cm viewpoint, when the dog leaves without approaching him, he has maintained his safety with that behaviour. He's a winner in his mind and next time he feels awkward and anxious he will use that same technique again.

Interestingly though, I have been in a position where He's been on the lead and another dog has too, I have let Chips off and he's ran the other way. Chips doesn't want to practice defensive acts, he's done it when he feels there was no other choice. When there's choice, he makes a good one and goes the other way. He has made lots of new friends by learning a good approach, and that he doesn't need to practice defensiveness. Yet had I dragged him past dog after dog, whilst he ranted and raved, his behaviour would be stronger than ever.

A Series of Choices

Just like Chips in this scenario, your own dog's behaviour is determined by his choices. Dogs have few choices in the world we have brought them into. We choose most things for them and we try to do our best to make the right ones, because we love them. I'm not sure there's anyone that has ever loved a dog who hasn't thought at least once, "I wish you could tell me what you want".

We can enable and empower our dogs though, by ensuring they choose as many things as they want to, in their lives. For example, I empower Chips by practicing off lead walking around but not too close to other dogs, he gets the chance to look at them and then the choice to follow me. That natural choice for him was set up so he can make the right one – following me – whilst lack of choice would be keeping him on a tight lead whilst he ranted, because he had no other choice in his mind. It took some time to do this with him though, and a series of set-ups for him to make the right choices, so don't just let your dog off the lead if he rants.

It will be easier for you to understand how simple canine coaching is, by viewing it as a series of choices for your dog. Then we attach a favourable consequence to the good and useful choices, whilst tweaking the environment to make the less useful choices less accessible.

For example; if your dog jumps up. For attention, he has probably learned that jumping leads to your attention. Any type of interaction with you is better than none – because you are the centre of his world. So, whilst you may sigh, say no and push him off, your dog just sees you looking at him and touching him, which is a pretty powerful reward for any human focussed dog. Compare that to being ignored if he doesn't jump up and you can see how easily the choice to jump up is made and reinforced.

You can tweak the choices and consequence to change the act of jumping up and empower your dog at the same time. This is what we are going to cover during the missions in this book.

Choices are routes in the mind. We all have these routes, humans and dogs alike. In fact, all sentient beings have the capacity for choice. Here's an analogy of choices and how your dog makes them:

Imagine a meadow surrounded by a high wall, the grass on

the meadow is high too, probably up to your dog's knees. There are three exit points, gates along one wall and no other way of getting out of the meadow. Your dog hears you call him and has to choose whether to come or not, his choice will be made initially based on how motivated he is to come when you call. He looks across the field and can see you stood behind one of the gates. The other gate has a friendly looking dog and the third gate is another meadow. Your dog has to make a choice so runs towards the gate which motivates him most of all. As he runs, he flattens the grass and gets to your gate for a reward and a game.

Now imagine this is repeated ten times, the grass will be quite flat by now and the easiest route to take will be the one that comes directly to you, add that to your successful motivation and your dog has learned to make the right choice, the pathway through the flat grass is set and you are the rewarding consequence.

Now go back to the first time your dog made the choice and imagine that you were less interesting than the gate with the friendly dog behind it. So even though you are calling your dog, he chooses a different gate. You decide to try again, without changing your own offering, so your dog makes the same choice again, then repeatedly until the easiest, trodden pathway leads away from you and to the other dog.

This describes how neural pathways work when your dog learns. This is what the out of control dog at the park has done, the one who is shouted constantly by their human but still running at every dog that he sees.

If we replace the trodden grass for well used routes in a dog's brain, we can see exactly why the most practiced route is the easiest one for the dog to take, along with why we need to make the favourable choice the easiest one for the dog, by enhancing motivation and tweaking consequences.

Mission One. Motivation and Markers

The first mission in the guide is designed to lay the foundation for everything we do afterwards. Learning what motivates your dog and introduction of a marker, for good choices.

A marker is something that tells your dog that they made the right choice. A natural marker is delivering a food reward, but dogs do multiple things very quickly and it's easy to miss the exact point that we want to reinforce, so a marker is used to pinpoint the choice.

Using a marker makes timing easier, because it helps us to mark the exact choice we want to reinforce, with one single, known sound. The sound is paired in your dog's mind with his motivating reward. Then it has the ultimate power for reinforcing choices to change them from awkward ones to excellent ones.

What is a motivating reward? That depends on your dog and what he likes best.

Your dog will be motivated by something unique to him. Markers are generally paired with food reward, because food reward triggers dopamine. It's also extremely powerful because food is required to keep the dog alive, so it's an important reinforcer due to its high importance to survival.

Choosing Food Rewards

The type of food you use will depend on your dog's preferences. One of mine loves a reward of peas or butter beans, whilst the others spit it back, looking offended. The more your dog likes the food that you are using for a reward, the more motivated he will be. Don't go straight for the one that drives your dog demented with expectation and glee though, because you will be using your secret weapon much sooner than you should.

I suggest you test a few food types by seeing how excited your dog gets when you produce them. The keener he is, the more that particular food will motivate your friend. Then choose five or six on a sliding scale that you can alternate depending on whether your dog needs a boost.

The image below shows an example of how to scale food reward to task. It's important to have options with food reward, where your dog has sufficient interest to learn for food low on the scale, but you have options for that motivation boost, if he needs it.

Important note: when choosing food rewards beware of highly processed dog food and treats. There are a lot of scary ingredients in dog treats, colours, preservatives and chemicals that could change how your dog feels and acts, all on their own. Watch out for heavily marketed treats with long chemical names in the composition area. Just like colourings and preservatives affect the biological brain health of people, they affect dogs. So, at best case scenario bad treats will make focus more difficult for your dog and at worst case, adversely affect their long-term health.

Choosing A Marker

Choosing a marker also depends on your dog. You can use one marker or many, I suggest you start with one as we work through the first few missions at least, just to keep things consistent in the early stages.

A word you don't usually use is a good marker, be careful of this though because when your dog has learned that the marker leads to food you must always provide a treat when you use the word, for optimal results. I use the marker, "good" during some fun sessions at home and the dogs know it when we are walking too. So, if they make a nice choice when on a walk, I can accidently mark it with "good boy" and am instantly the focus of at least four expectant eyes and have to produce something for them to eat. Rewarding a marker is particularly important if you want to maintain its power after an initial pairing of marker to reward.

The beauty of using a marker word is that you can use tone and inflection in delivery. If your dog gets over excited regularly and is very animated, you can use a calm tone to deliver your marker, along with calm, quiet movements during coaching. Your dog will respond to your own sounds and movement, so if you move quietly and steadily, your dog will be more settled too.

If your dog is low in confidence you can deliver the marker with excitement. Move yourself around with some animation and your dog's energy will become more animated too.

A classic marker is a clicker. The clicker is a neutral sound created by a small box that you click with your thumb. Clickers are great, as they really pinpoint the moment that the choice is made. Some dogs don't like the sound though, which can be counter-productive, wrapping it in a towel might help with that, but it's not really convenient when out and about. If your dog doesn't like the sound of the clicker – perhaps you could practice a tongue click instead. With marker use, anything goes – if it's consistent and always rewarded.

Making the Connection

Connecting a marker to your dog's motivation of choice (the food) is pretty straightforward. It's just a case of following the marker with the food until your dog knows that the sound leads to food delivery.

It usually takes a few short sessions of marker and food reward before your dog is fully aware that one leads to the other.

What you need:

1. A consistent marker, such as a word, clicker or other sound.
2. Many tiny tasty treats. The tastier the treats, the more powerful the connection will be with the marker. They should be large enough to taste and small enough to swallow without chewing. The brief taste will leave your dog wanting more, whereas a big chunk to chew is distracting and filling, so your dog will get full and bored more easily.

This task is best carried out in an area that your dog knows really well, such as at home or in your garden. Distractions such as sniffs, passers-by, sounds and other stimulators should be avoided when teaching anything new. Remember the choice gates in the meadow? Set your coaching sessions up so that the gate with you behind it is the most fascinating one, make yourself interesting and your food offerings irresistible.

Position yourself so you are and offer the most tempting thing in the area, you can't go wrong.

Coaching Steps

1. Sit on the ground, or a chair if your dog gets over excited with you on the ground, with your treats and marker at the ready.
2. Let your dog explore the area first if you have just gone into it.
3. Wait until your dog is either considering what to do next or glances at you, then deliver the marker and one bit of food, five times in a row.
4. Throw a bit of food across the room so that your dog goes to fetch it.
5. Repeat steps three and four – three to five times depending on how interested and happy your dog is, then end the session.

After doing a few sessions your dog should be naturally aware that the sound of his marker provides a treat. You can test this by being in a normal area – free from distractions and waiting until he's not looking and delivering it, if your dog comes for his treat, the connection is made. If he doesn't come when he hears the sound, your dog hasn't made the connection yet, you maybe need to do one more session.

When the connection is made there are two important things to remember:

The sound will reinforce whatever your dog is doing at the time it's delivered. So, if he's jumping up or running away and you use the marker, you have made that particular behaviour stronger, by reinforcing it. Your dog will repeat that behaviour, without a doubt.

Secondly, always use the marker with food. If you use it and don't give food, the sound will lose its power. Your dog will stop bothering with it, and you have undone all the work you carried out when you were pairing the sound with its real power source – the food.

Mission Accomplished

Your first mission is accomplished when your dog knows exactly what the marker means and comes directly to you expecting a treat when you mark a nice choice that he makes. The choice can be anything from looking your way on a walk, to keeping all four feet on the ground when he might otherwise jump up.

When we use a marker, we can use it with one or more of the following approaches:

1. Marking/Capture means that we use the sound to

capture any choice the dog makes, that we appreciate.

2. Luring is the act of showing the dog what we would like, then we capture the act by marking it with a click.

3. Shaping is teaching a choice via a few different smaller choices and marking each one. This works well when building the confidence of a worried dog.

Capturing Choices

When you have an established marker, start to use it to reinforce your dog's good choices, on a regular basis. Think of it like you're capturing something special that you dog chose to do by taking a snapshot with your marker. Capture everything you want your dog to repeat. It's a good idea to put bowls of small treats around your home so you will always have one to hand. Then if your dog does something you like, mark and reward the choice, then he will repeat that choice because it's been reinforced.

One of the things we can all do if we don't focus is ignore good choices from our dogs or not notice them at all. We then notice the bad choices because they are inconvenient to us. This is quite sad for the dog who is only trying things to see which choices work, after all. If a choice has no consequence, your dog is likely not to practice it anymore, instead favouring a choice that makes something interesting or rewarding happen.

A typical example of ignoring good choices is when the dog

checks in with his human on a walk. Checking in is a wonderful choice, because it reinforces the bond between the dog and his human. The dog looks back and makes brief eye contact, the person acknowledges the dog's effort and the walk continues.

Many dogs check in initially but are ignored, so they stop bothering and just wander along on their own. We people like our screens and it seems to be a default option to pull out your phone on a walk. If your dog checks in with you, but you're looking at a screen and don't acknowledge him, he's more likely to go off and approach other dogs and people instead. This will naturally put him, or the unknown dogs he approaches, in danger. It will also be terrible for his self-esteem and your relationship. Our dogs have short little lives, so we need to embrace them as often as we can, because one day we won't be able to.

Important note on checking in: some dogs check in naturally all the time. These dogs may be genetically visual, such as the collie or shepherd breeds. Some may be quite seriously attached to their human and desperately want confirmation of that bond, as often as possible. It's important to find a balance with checking in. Too much and the dog will lose the freedom they naturally get during a walk, and too little will give the dog no reason to check in at all.

Takeaway Points

- Our role as caretakers and friends of domestic dogs is to manage their lives so well that they have a good experience.
- The first step of understanding is total observation.
- When dogs learn through coaching, they are becoming empowered along the way.
- Behaviour is a series of choices, and each choice will be repeated if it produces a consequence that the dog likes.
- If a dog is ignored when he makes a helpful choice, he will usually not do it again, based on the lack of interesting result.
- By making the result of helpful choices the most rewarding in the area, the dog will choose it more often.
- Your dog will choose his own motivation.

Part Three:
Fun and Focus

Before we begin any more practical steps, we are going to take a look at communication. It's important to know that our dogs are happy and having fun when they learn, for the reasons we already know.

Canine body language tells us a great deal when we focus on it and know what to look for. Like people, dogs have personalities of their own and their own unique communication styles. There are some universal signs that tell us how a dog feels and we can learn a lot from them.

Take some time to observe and learn your dog's neutral state. How does your dog look when he's not showing any strong emotion such as fear or excitement? Where do his ears sit on his head, how do his eyes look, and what position is his tail in? A lot of this will depend on his breed type — my little Pomeranian cross, for example, has a tail held high over her beautiful self, and when it drops there's something wrong with her for sure.

Here's another example of a tail that's neutral and high. This little dog also looks happy and is doing a dog smile, has ears pricked forward and a relaxed face.

But if my Jack Russell terrier holds his tail as high as our little Pomeranian lady, he's far from feeling neutral and is probably highly aroused by something in the environment. This picture shows an aroused dog with a hard stare and high tail. His body also looks quite tense as he is deciding how to react.

Even though the first dogs have higher tails, the dogs show very different intent, which is exactly why you need to pinpoint your own dog's neutral body language and work from there.

Tails, ears and posture are three of the easiest things to read in a dog's body language.

A tail that goes below neutral can dictate fear or anxiety, and how much is directly related to how low the tail drops. If it goes above neutral and high behind the dog, like a flag, the dog is usually aroused and interested in something. He may even be offering conflict. Think of a high tail like a flag — the higher the tail is from its neutral position, the bolder or more aroused a dog feels.

The dog's ear position is again based on neutral. There are many ear shapes, so exactly how your dog's ears look will depend on his neutral position. Generally, the further back the dog's ears go on their head, the more uncomfortable the dog feels. If he can't pull his ears back because they are floppy or heavy, the same attempt is made but the ears pinch to the side of the head instead. Ear shape is linked with facial tension.

This dog's ears are pulled right back, and his eyes and face are tense. The Pomeranian shown above and this tense dog here are similar breed types, so their neutral ear position is one of pricked ears like the Pom's. This dog, however, shows extreme anxiety because his ears are pulled towards the back of his head – as far from neutral position as possible. This position is sometimes called seal ears.

Posture is measured by how loose or tense the dog's body is. A neutral posture is relaxed and shows no tension. A happy dog that's enjoying himself will be loose and relaxed from his nose to the tip of his tail. He may be wriggly and smiling. Here's a loose-bodied, happy dog who is very pleased with life and smiling all over his face.

A scared dog will tense up, try to avoid conflict and crouch with the tail and rear tucked under, in an attempt look smaller. A confrontational dog, on the other hand, will tense up but try to look bigger. The tension is because they are worried about something in the environment. Whether they respond by fight or flight will depend on their prior experiences and learning, plus their personality.

Mission Two. Spotting Neutral

Your own dog's neutral position is unique to their body shape and breed type. Whilst you probably already have an idea of their general, neutral stance and the way they look when they are happy or sad, it's good to start looking for the smaller signals of change, too.

I can confidently say that canine coaching is 90% observation and the other 10% is split between timing, understanding and empathy.

Signs of Confusion

Calming signals are the name given to behaviour changes, by Turid Rugaas. As a natural behaviour, calming signals are split into two types or can also be described as mild or extreme. Some people simply call them signs of anxiety or stress.

A dog will use these signs to show other dogs, people and other animals that it means no harm and is trying hard to defuse any kind of tension. The dog can also use them to calm himself, even when left completely alone. It can be either conscious or unconscious, depending on the situation and the individual dog.

When we try to teach dogs something new, we must look out for calming signals, to check for any signals of worry or stress.

Mild signs of stress can include:

- A big nose lick
- Glancing away and back
- Lip licking
- Looking to the distance
- Pulling back the lips, maybe in a submissive grin
- Sitting down and lifting a front paw
- Yawning

It's important as we work through the missions that you look out for these signs and change your tactics if they start to appear, because it means the dog is feeling pressured or confused. If the basic mild calming signals do not alleviate the feeling of anxiety, by being properly accepted and adapted to, and the dog continues to feel anxious or stressed, other calming signals will appear.

These can include:

- Cowering
- Drooling
- Dropping to the ground either rolling on his back or crouching over his stomach
- Freezing, maybe tucking the tail
- Panting
- Urinating
- Walking slowly

These later signals should honestly never appear when a dog is learning. We need to notice the milder signals and react by changing the approach, taking a break or making the lesson clearer to the dog. They usually occur when we ask too much, too soon.

Dogs use body language to express confusion, commonly called displacement behaviour. It means the dog is experiencing two conflicting thoughts or emotions, such as a desire to please but also anxiety because he doesn't know how or what is expected of him.

Common displacement behaviours include sniffing the floor, fetching a toy, some calming signals, even snuffling and sneezing. Dogs may scratch themselves as if they have a serious itch, pace around or try to get you to play. If the lesson is not changed at this point, the dog's confidence will seriously drop. He may start to show appeasement signals such as licking and crouching, dropping his eyes and head, or rolling on his back. At this point, stop pushing your dog and switch to something easier. He obviously doesn't have a clue of what is required of him, so let the dog succeed and play.

Mission Accomplished

This mission is accomplished when you have written the following five points down and committed them to your memory, for use in all canine coaching sessions and everywhere you go with your dog.

Your dog's neutral:

1. Posture
2. Ear position
3. Tail position

Then:

4. What happens when your dog gets tense?
5. How do you know that your dog is happy?

Keep observing your dog for any signs of change in how he feels, and you will start to notice the things that catch his attention on walks and how he responds to them. If he looks a bit anxious when learning, he will drop from neutral, and if he's having fun, he will rise from his neutral position and smile.

Mission Three. Watch Me

At this point, we begin using our marker and the observation we have learned to teach cued choices. The cue is a word that we attach to a choice, via a careful learning process so that the dog knows what the cue means, and what we would like him to do.

Mission three is a prelude to all other cued choices because it's important that you have your dog's attention before you ask him to do something.

We often see people talking to their dog, who is totally engaged in something else and takes no notice of the requests he is given. It's no one's fault really — it's just that both the dog and his human are not in a place where they can properly communicate and understand each other. That is where canine coaching comes in.

Sadly though, when people talk to their dog who is otherwise engaged in something entirely different, the dog usually gets the blame for not responding. Dogs are called ignorant, stubborn and even dominant because they refuse to engage. Oftentimes, they get punished for not listening, which can lead to even less engagement because the dog becomes scared and tries to hide or leave.

The 'watch me' cue is wonderful for engagement. We can use it to get the attention of our dog, or as part of play and mutual enjoyment. This is a great relationship and bond builder.

All you need to teach this cue is a marker, some food reward and a toy that your dog likes. If he doesn't particularly like classic toys, that's fine, just use the food.

You can teach this cue in the following steps:

1. Sit on the ground if possible, facing your dog. If not, sit on a chair as the idea is to make your face as accessible as possible to your dog.
2. When your dog looks into your face naturally, mark quickly and give a food reward.
3. If he doesn't naturally look into your face, you can offer a small lure such as a squeak from your lips or bring your hand over your head then down behind the back of your head until your dog's eyes hit yours, then mark the choice to look at you.
4. Practice steps one to three a few times.
5. Introduce the cue directly after the marker then bring the cue forward until it is delivered before the marker and then start to deliver it before your dog meets your eyes.
6. Practice these steps over a few sessions in a quiet area, then gradually increase distractions at a pace your dog can cope with. Don't ask too much too soon, and always ensure that your dog can handle any added distractions before asking him to watch you on cue. When you move to new areas, it's a good idea to use higher value rewards, to ensure you're still the most interesting thing when your dog is learning to watch you.

The most important point is to have fun. Don't keep asking your dog to do the same thing over and over in one session. If he's got it, play a game to cement that new knowledge in his mind. It can be tempting to ask over and over again when a dog is learning a cue. However, forced repetition is counter-productive and will cause confusion or lack of confidence. Carrying out two good cued choices and a game is much more useful, and play has been proven to build memories in dogs, more so than simple repetition.

Cues

A quick recap on cues and how to introduce them, establishing them as an associated term to a choice.

Firstly, we make an association between the cue and the choice by delivering it after the marker.

CHOICE **+** CAPTURE WITH MARKER **+** CUE **=** REWARD

Then we strengthen the association by delivering it before the marker.

CHOICE **+** CUE **+** CAPTURE WITH MARKER **=** REWARD

Then we begin to deliver the cue before the dog makes the choice and soon the dog knows exactly what it means.

CUE **+** CHOICE **+** CAPTURE WITH MARKER **=** REWARD

The rate at which you bring the cue forward depends on how quickly your dog gets the idea.

Mission Accomplished

This mission is completed when your dog can watch you on cue at home and in the garden. It may take three to six sessions of around ten minutes to get to this point. Remember not to expect too much too soon, or your dog will lose his self-confidence. So, take your time and have fun.

Proofing

Proofing a choice means making it the easiest choice in any situation. Basically, we make the cued choice environment proof, often called generalisation. This is something that can't be rushed. Any dog that can do something perfectly at home will struggle when out in the environment, because everything looks and smells differently — there are simply too many distractions. Think about moving into a new neighbourhood as you slowly get accustomed to your surroundings.

To proof a choice, we make one thing harder at a time. We also raise motivation when we make it harder, by using special rewards when we ask something new and tough from our dogs. It's a good idea to re-teach a cued choice, briefly with the first few environmental changes as this will raise your dog's self-belief and not expect too much from him.

Successful proofing alternates the following points, to teach the dog his choice in all environments he goes to.

- Increase the time your dog holds the cue. For example, in the beginning of the 'watch me' cue, a brief glance is fine. Then you can withhold the marker and reward for increasing moments until your dog has learned to hold your gaze for much longer. Then you can release the dog's gaze by marker and reward delivery.
- Change the environment by adding in reasonable distractions, then re-teach your dog the cue. Start with a quiet field and build to a busy park. Remember to raise your reward and drop your expectations of long cued eye contact at this point. Always raise difficulty of one thing at a time, and ensure the right choice is always the easiest one.
- Change reward delivery and timing as your dog learns the choice in real time.

Food Reward Delivery

Delivery of your marker and food reward can be used to teach then strengthen a choice.

At the beginning in the very early stages of learning the choice, you can use continuous rewards, which means you pay out regularly and quickly to show your dog that he's doing exactly the right thing for the best possible result. So make sure your deliveries are quick during continuous reward stages.

When your dog is making the choice unprompted, you can change the delivery of your marker and subsequent reward to make it less frequent. This acknowledges that your dog has learned but is not yet fully competent. This reward delivery type is called variable reward and is great for choice reinforcement. A little like a slot machine that pays out often but small, so we keep trying until we get a big pay out. Remember that it's your marker that's variable. So, don't ever mark then not reward because your marker will lose its appeal. Just gradually withdraw your marker as your dog starts to consistently make the right choice.

Optimism

Canine coaching sets a dog up to succeed by delivering a lesson in manageable steps without expecting too much too soon. This keeps the dog's confidence nice and high, which is excellent for learning. A confident dog will try new things, stay optimistic and happy, which yields the best possible outcome for his efforts. However, if he gets it wrong, gets confused or senses that you are even the least bit frustrated, your dog's body language will change and he will become pessimistic. A dog in a pessimistic state yields the worst possible results for his efforts, will often expect to fail and may not even try at all.

You can boost your dog's optimism by teaching simple-steps

lessons, avoiding too much repetition, making the right choices the easiest ones for him and celebrating his achievements every step of the way until he becomes an optimistic genius.

Takeaway Points

- Coaching must always be fun for the dog.
- Every dog has a neutral body and face position that we see when they are experiencing no strong emotions.
- A happy dog will smile, and is loose and relaxed.
- A worried dog is tense and holds his body tight.
- Confrontational dogs make themselves bigger.
- Non-confrontational dogs make themselves smaller.
- Confused dogs show specific behaviours called calming signals or displacement behaviour.
- Play increases learning.
- Proofing increases the ability for dogs to make correct choices.
- A dog that takes an optimistic view of learning will expect good things and try new things with natural confidence. A dog with low confidence may take a pessimistic view and avoid trying new things due to lack of self-belief.
- We can create optimism by setting our dogs up to succeed and rewarding them when they do.

Part Four: Useful Cues

Now that we have achieved a good base of knowledge on canine coaching, we can teach some cues that make life easier for you and your dog. For this area, I have chosen useful cues as opposed to ones that may have been traditionally taught in the past.

Alternate Your Tasks

Alternating tasks is something you can do when your dog has learned a few different cues, whilst he is learning new ones. If you ask your dog to do something new and difficult followed by something else new and difficult, it will knock your dog's confidence.

Use a ping-pong effect with your teaching.

Start with something easy, play, switch to a new and tougher lesson, play, then finish with something easy followed by your final game. If your dog is keen to carry on, do one more ping-pong but remember that it's easy to go beyond your dog's capacity and interest so it's better to stop a moment early than to push beyond a successful session and then regret it.

The following visual is a good blueprint for coaching that covers a ping-pong approach to teaching. If you coach every day, using this as your guide will give the quickest results.

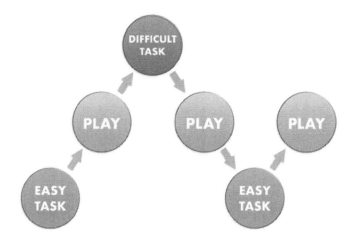

A few tips to remember as you coach:

- Every session should begin after your dog has had the chance to toilet and check out the coaching area. So, don't go straight to the park and start coaching — allow your dog a few minutes of freedom to sniff, toilet settle and then do a little coaching.
- Start your sessions with an easy cue, to get your dog keen and confident to learn the next big thing.
- All sessions should end on a good note. End your lesson on a high and your dog will be happy and

brimming with confidence.

- Sessions should take no longer than 15 minutes. Shorter sessions are even better. It's better to do a 5-minute session that's good than to push on for longer whilst the dog is bored and confused.
- Sessions should always be fun. If you don't feel like coaching one day, don't do it! Your dog will know that you're not completely engaged, and he will feel bad too.
- End everything with a game. Play has been proven to make learning much easier, so split your session between play and learning — then always finish with play.

Mission Four. Hand Press

The hand press is an extension of targeting which can be used for husbandry jobs such as visits to the vets and nail clipping. Your dog will literally learn to press his nose into the palm of your open hand until you release him with the marker and reward. The choice can be strengthened so much that your dog will be so focused on the press that a vet can examine him without too much stress.

It needs to be taught as targeting first, then strengthened via shaping. We teach this early, because it will help with things like recall and jumping up throughout the other missions.

Hand press can be taught by following the steps below:

- This lesson can start with a lure to your palm and capture when your dog touches your hand, or it can be a simple capture if the dog has any interest in touching your hand with his nose. With the lure, you simply place your hand, palm up on the floor, or at your dog's nose height, then place a treat on top of it.
- When your dog gets the treat and inadvertently touches your hand, mark and give him another treat.
- Do this a few times and then progress to just pretending to put a treat onto your hand, but still click as your dog touches your palm.
- Next, you can include a cue word as the dog touches the you. Then, move your hand around and click as your dog follows it and touches you with his nose.
- After the dog is totally confident to touch you with his nose, start to withhold the marker. Do this carefully because if you move on too soon, your dog will lose confidence and will be less capable of learning.
- The idea is to withhold the click, shaping the behaviour of keeping his nose on your hand for longer each time. With a dog that finds this difficult, a simple shaping session would focus on shorter touches, followed by longer touches until the dog really presses his nose into the palm of your hand.

The steps are adaptable depending on the individual dog. Your dog may fly through them, miss some out because the he is finding them too easy, or get stuck on some because they are too hard. If you get stuck, then simply make things easier by going back to a step that the dog finds easy in order to rebuild the foundation knowledge and ability.

When you teach the hand press, remember to use your cue in the way we previously covered.

By the time it's taught, you have also taught your dog the basis of targeting. Now you can follow the same steps to target your dog to anything you wish. For example, a soft keyring with its own cue word, in case you ever drop your keys on a walk, and your dog can find them. You could name his toys and target him to each one, or even teach him to fetch the remote control for the TV. Simply replace the final touch and press by shaping the act of picking the item up instead and bringing it back to you. It's a good idea not to teach the hand press and retrieve too close together as your dog may be confused as to whether he's supposed to press or pick up. Perhaps got through a couple more missions after teaching the hand press before teaching a targeting for retrieve.

Mission Accomplished

This mission is accomplished when your dog will press his nose into your hand on cue then hold it there for five full seconds. After this mission is accomplished, remember to proof the choice in many different areas, building distractions gradually.

Mission Five. Get Moving

After your dog has learned to touch your hand on cue, you can use it for fun, recall and as general targeting to your hand for teaching more elaborate cues. Mission five is a fun one to get your dog moving and get his energy flowing. You can carry this out alone or with someone else.

The cue is yours to choose but ensure it varies enough from the hand press cue, to prevent confusing your dog.

1. Go into a spacious area, maybe the garden or a field, and offer your dog your palm to touch. When he does, use a different cue from the hand press and release immediately with the marker and reward.

2. Next, run away from your dog as quickly as possible until you are a few metres away, then offer your palm again, with the new cue. When he runs to you and touches, mark and reward immediately.
   Or:
   Have another person that your dog knows offer their hand and give the cue, making their hand obvious, then mark and reward instantly. This might need to begin within a couple of metres of your own position and make the distance further over time.

3. Repeat step two five or six times and finish with a game.

4. Getting the dog moving is great for confidence and this mission is particularly good for building self-belief,

and the fun and extra movement gets the dog's energy flowing just as play does.

The engagement associated with this mission is wonderful. It's a great relationship builder, a new cue that can be used to call your dog back, and generally great fun for everyone involved. The movement benefits us too, releasing feel-good endorphins that provide happy and positive feelings.

Mission Accomplished

This mission is complete when you have carried out ten full sessions of this exercise, either between you and your dog, with another person whilst your dog runs between you, or as a mixture of the two. Enjoy this mission — it's designed to feel great and get you playing like you did as a child — just for the sake of it.

Mission Six. Come When Called

Recall is one of the most common problems that people have with their dogs. Calling a dog that won't come when you ask, or even acknowledge you, can be frustrating and embarrassing.

Excellent recall prevents associated embarrassment. Most of all though, it is safe and prevents accident, fights and your dog harassing other dogs, even if he's just being friendly. Many people have dogs that shouldn't be approached on walks — they may be old, ill, scared or defensive.

Running free is every dog's right and really good for them, too. They should run free and enjoy themselves. They should also come back when called for everyone's sake. Teaching a good recall is fundamental for positive walks; we do it by teaching them a recall cue and making sure that coming back is the most motivating choice. We can't just let them free on walks and hope they come back because we have some tasty food and a toy — we need to build and proof the cue like any other mission.

The good news is that you can utilise the hand touch now, to help with recall. If you have been running around and playing with your dog, or he has been running between you and another person, you already have a head start. Your dog should associate running to you with all the best rewards. We just need to go through the steps of making sure your dog makes the right choice, then strengthening that choice until it's the only one.

We first start to teach in the most boring areas, building to areas of high distraction gradually and always setting the dog up to succeed. We do this with tempting rewards for motivation and by creating an environment in which your dog will both make the easiest and best choice.

The following steps are a guide to teaching flawless recall, even if your dog has got into the habit of ignoring you to this point:

1. Decide your motivator; it's a good idea to go for a high value food reward but not the most favourite, as we will need that as we use distractions. Consider other motivators to add strength to the food reward, too. Some dogs really like squeaky toys, so perhaps have a special toy that only comes out for recall and goes back at the end of every practice. To get recall right, it's important to be rewarding and remain calm. If the dog is not responding to his name when we are kind, he certainly won't improve as a result of anger or frustration.

2. Decide your cue. You can use your dog's name for this if you want to, then add 'come' or something similar at the end. A word or a whistle or the dog's name all work fine. Start by sitting with the dog and have your food reward available. Once your dog looks at you, use the cue word (we'll use 'come' for this example) and immediately reward the dog. Repeat this a number of times but make sure the dog isn't losing interest.

3. The second stage requires a little trickery. We are going to use the dog's own actions to make them believe they were coming anyway. As soon as the dog begins walking towards you, make yourself the most attractive thing in the room and encourage him to get there as soon as possible. As soon as he is too close to escape, repeat the cue word 'come' and instantly reward. This method allows the dog's choices to become part of the process, which makes for a solid learning experience.

4. For this step, be in an environment with enough space

for both of you to move a couple of metres in any direction. A back yard will usually do just fine. With the dog on the lead, we begin by repeating step 1 a couple of times to promote the idea of what is happening. It's something familiar and also helps with proofing. Next, we begin to walk away from the dog, just a few steps at first, as soon as he begins to follow, use the 'come' cue and reward as soon as he arrives. Repeat this process and slowly build to longer distances. If the dog seems confident and relaxed, we can add running away to this step but make sure the lead is used safely.

5. By this stage, we should have built up a pretty good response from the dog to the cue word 'come'. Making sure of this in a way that did not allow failure was an important part of building the dog's confidence to succeed. It is a good idea at this stage to change the treat to something with a stronger smell and better taste to aid motivation. Still working from a lead in a big space, allow the dog to wander away. When he is a few steps away, say 'come'. The dog should return immediately for his treat. Repeat this step and allow for longer distances. Be careful not to call the dog in the middle of some other behaviour (such as toileting or sniffing something interesting).

6. After a lot of careful practice around the home and garden, we can move outdoors to a local park or open space. With the dog still on a lead, use steps 3 and 4 in

this new environment. If your dog is likely to run away, even if you're not sure of their complete attention, use a long training lead. Slowly build up the length of lead to allow more freedom. If you can see that the dog is distracted, stop using the cue word. We want him to be 100% sure about what "come"means.

7. Go right back to the beginning but this time take the lead away. If at any point the dog does not return, during this stage, go back to using the lead until you are confident, he has got it. Go through steps 1-5 again and proof the behaviour without the lead. Take care if you intend to do this in a public space. At this stage, a tempting distraction may be too much to overcome.

Now that your dog is becoming an expert, you can begin to use the cue word in new environments and even introduce new people to say 'come'. As before, begin with on-the-lead coaching and follow the same steps.

Whilst the steps above are a blueprint for excellent recall, there are some extra coaching skills that will help too, particularly if you're teaching this to a dog that doesn't always respond when called.

First, use your voice with real wisdom. We often see people shouting their dog's name from a good distance, whilst the dog looks totally oblivious to their efforts. I have never once seen a dog hear their name called on the umptieth try and suddenly decide that they have brilliant recall — bombing back to their person like their return was never questioned in the first place. What usually happens is the dog stops listening altogether, whilst their human's voice gets further from them as they run.

When learning recall, dogs have an invisible perimeter around them and their human. If they stay within this perimeter, recall will always succeed, because the choice to come back when called is at a distance they have learned. If, however, the dog goes beyond that perimeter, they are likely not to come back to the first or the twentieth call, particularly if there's something exciting in the distance. If your dog was to go beyond his perimeter and towards something interesting, you can be sure you have expected too much too soon, and after the second time you call him, you need to stop calling him and do something else. Each time a dog runs through their human's voice, they are creating a habit of it and will more likely run through the same voice again. The best prevention of this choice is not to expect too much too soon.

After trying the voice and if your dog loves a squeaker, perhaps pull out the toy and squeak that. It might be just the motivation your dog needs to come back. As soon as he turns and looks, make yourself exciting and your dog might choose to come running back. Don't fall into the trap of calling and squeaking all over the place though, if your dog isn't listening. If the same tactic doesn't work on the second attempt, do something else.

Another little trick you can try is running the other way. If your dog looks at you but considers going further from you, that look is pure gold. It's your chance to be overwhelmingly exciting. Use a high voice and run in the other direction and your dog is likely to come after you, as you have suddenly become more interesting than everything else in the area.

Mission Accomplished

Your mission is complete when your dog comes right back on your first call in five different areas.

Mission Seven. Loose Lead and Easy Walks

I spoke to someone recently that said they had stopped walking their dog because he pulled so much on walks. What a sad situation that is, particularly when a dog has lived with their family since puppyhood. Dogs love walks, the only exception is stressed or worried dogs who benefit from less outside time because the world is a scary place.

A dog pulling on the lead makes that choice because it's his most natural behaviour. No animal is born on a tether and if we put a tether on, we must also include guidance on how to act when tethered – for the dog.

The first thing we consider when a dog pulls on walks is what they are wearing. A collar or slip collar around the neck of a pulling dog is a recipe for throat pain and injury. The dog's throat is a tender area and – in my opinion – collars should be reserved for dogs that never pull or discarded altogether.

The worst use of collars is by trainers and those giving advice that a certain collar is the key to solving a dog's behaviour. For example, a tightening chain or even a chain with prongs on that push into the dog's skin when they pull. Another collar type is one that uses electricity to change behaviour, which is thankfully becoming gradually banned in most European countries.

The idea behind a collar like the ones I have mentioned here is that they make the dog change their choices via the threat of pain. They don't really teach a different choice though or start off with a good lesson because the dog has to practice the behaviour before the pain is delivered.

So, what we have in this situation is a dog that has never been taught to relax on the lead. We then bring in a collar that's supposed to change that dog's behaviour. The dog then pulls as he always does, but this time, he gets hurt, getting punished for doing something that no-one has asked him not to do. The punishment has been delivered by his most trusted human or a stranger whilst his human looks on. How very sad is that?

There is a much nicer option though, an obvious one if we look at it carefully. It could still involve changing walking equipment but this time to something kinder, a harness. There are a range of harnesses available now; however, some scary looking harnesses with areas that tighten in vulnerable places should be avoided. Most are comfortable though and redistribute the dog's weight to make walking less of a struggle for the human and often naturally stop pulling. A good harness will fit around less vulnerable body areas, and be comfortable and kind to the dog. If you have a dog that pulls on a collar, it's worth considering a harness instead.

When we have the walking equipment right, we can begin teaching the dog not to pull. To make the choice of a loose lead because it's rewarding and motivating to do that. Like everything we have learned on this journey so far, we are aiming for helpful choice that's easy and has the best consequences.

First, change the routine. A new routine is a good idea to teach a new skill. If you usually go out of the front door and get dragged to the park down the road by an excited dog, don't start trying to teach a loose lead at the moment you leave the house because your dog will be highly excited and less likely to learn something new. Time your lesson wisely and you will get to the desired point much more quickly. It is wise to begin teaching this lesson during or after a walk, particularly if your dog is high on energy. Trying to teach a loose lead with a dog that's brimming with energy is unlikely to succeed.

We have already covered a few things that will help with this mission. By this point, your dog should be generally way more engaged with you. Be sure to have plenty of tiny food rewards and your chosen marker at the ready.

Then, it's just a case of implementing the following steps:

1. Ensure your dog is not full of energy. You can do this by giving him a loose run or walk before you begin.
2. Have your dog on the lead in an area of no to low distractions. Remember that we need to make this as easy as possible for him, to make your request his easiest choice to make.
3. Stand and wait, and if your dog is trying to pull you, wait until the lead goes slack then mark and reward your dog. It could take a while the first few times but if the area is dull enough, your dog will turn and ask what you're waiting for. This will slacken the lead

ready for your marker and reward.

4. When your dog gets the idea, he will start to slacken the lead quickly, because it's rewarding. Great! Keep delivering your marker and reward.

5. When you can stand together comfortably, start to move. Your dog may then pull to the end of the lead because it's what he's used to doing when you walk. At this point, change direction and use the words 'this way' as your dog turns with you, the lead will go slack. Mark and reward this natural good luck and practice.

6. Lengthen your sessions and practice facilitating a loose lead then marking it by changing direction a few times, using your 'this way' cue then ending the session with a game. Put the loose lead on cue too and your dog will start to relax his pulling.

Next, you can build time and distractions by proofing the new choice of walking without dragging you along. You already have a considerable toolkit to help if a big distraction comes along. You can ask for a hand touch, swiftly change direction whilst saying 'this way' or ask your dog to watch you until the distraction has passed by.

Another good thing to do — particularly if your dog is focused on things and reacts to them overtly — is to drop a few small bits of food on the ground for him to sniff out. Providing a distraction that overrules the interesting thing in the environment is key to having your dog choose what you want, rather than something else. It's all about the engagement and how interesting you are at the time.

Mission Accomplished

This mission can be considered completed when your dog walks nicely on the lead for a full ten minutes. It may take some time to get to this point, but ten minutes is a sweet spot and when you reach this, the rest will come naturally because you have laid the foundation for choosing a loose lead. Then you just need to continue to motivate it for a bit longer whilst adding distractions carefully during proofing.

Takeaway Points

- Always coach after a walk and give your dog the chance to explore the area and toilet.
- You can teach your dog any new choice by following a ping-pong approach.
- By following the diagram and only teaching one difficult choice per session, you will get to the desired point quicker and on excellent foundations.
- Don't rush teaching anything at all because the foundations are the most important step to learning new choices.
- If you move on too quickly, before the foundations are properly laid, the new behaviour will fall apart later on. Just as any structure would if it were built without foundations.
- Every behaviour is a choice; if you set up the environment to be conducive for your dog to make the right choices, then mark and reward them, and your dog will make them more often.
- Use your voice wisely.

Part Five:
Into the Future

Well done! By now, you should have a dog that makes excellent choices prompted by your own skill and understanding. The final area of this guide cover three more missions that you will find helpful in everyday life with your dog.

Mission Eight. Don't Jump Up.

Jumping up is another choice carried out because it's naturally rewarding to the dog. It's also something that can be changed easily by changing the consequences. The best approach to coaching a dog not to jump up is to teach an alternate choice and reward that one instead.

The most important thing to remember is that taking away the opportunity to practice jumping up will have the biggest effect on changing choices. Sometimes, people say ignore the jumping up and the behaviour will go away. But ignoring a practiced behaviour is far less effective than taking away the opportunity to practice altogether. The alternative choice will fill the gap in your dog's mind, where he would usually choose to jump up.

Here's how to do it:

1. The first thing to do is decide on a suitable alternative behaviour. It can be any choice that you put on cue. Common ones include sit, paw touch or even the position of having all four feet on the ground.

2. Teach the alternate choice with your marker and reward, add a cue to it the same way as usual, then practice and proof the choice on cue in any given situation. As your dog is most likely to jump up at home or on greeting the people that he likes best, you can cue the alternate choice early in the process and don't need to wait until it's proofed out and about.

3. When your dog knows the cued choice, you can use it just prior to when he would normally jump up. Mark and reward it, then give him all the attention he's asking for. Naturally, use your timing to get in first so the opportunity to jump is removed altogether. Because jumping up is an excited behaviour, make your attention slow and calm. Stroke him gently and keep your voice gentle — this should naturally calm his excitement to see you.

4. When you're sure your dog has settled down, you can end the greeting interaction.

5. Practice steps one to four every time you greet your dog. He will soon get the idea.

If your dog is a habitual jumper, it may take a little while to change this. The same rules apply though, easy chunks make good choices.

Jumping up is one behaviour that can easily be rewarded outside your control. Whilst it's lovely that other people like your dog, many people don't mind being jumped at and will reward it with attention. If it works, your dog will repeat it.

Extinction

Extinction is a coaching term that describes what happens to a practiced choice when the opportunity for the dog to practice it is taken away. The behaviour becomes extinct and is no longer practiced at all because it has ceased to be reinforced. Extinction is the place where all awkward choices can end up and be replaced by better ones.

If a choice has become extinct though and the dog suddenly gets the opportunity to practice it again, and it gets reinforced, the choice will be stronger than ever. So, if you have spent a few weeks setting your dog up for success by reinforcing a different choice, then he is encouraged to jump up and is rewarded just once, the behaviour will be back. For this reason, everyone in the home must be consistent with the coaching and the opportunity to jump up must be managed outside the home too.

For your interest, the term given to a returning choice that was previously extinct is spontaneous recovery.

Mission Accomplished

This mission will be completed when your dog has greeted you and/or others consistently a full five times without jumping up. If he jumps up once, even if he's carried out four successful alternate choices before that, you must start again from one.

This mission tests your skill more so rather than your dog's. If you coach with kindness and consistency, your dog will make the right choices and your coaching will show successful results.

Mission Nine. Happy Swapping

Swapping toys and other items including food is a crucial skill. A dog who learns that giving something up leads to getting something more interesting is a fantastic way to prevent resource guarding or even deal with the onset of it. Teaching to swap is also an excellent safety cue. If your dog gets hold of something that could do them harm, for example cooked chicken bones or something nasty at the park, a swap on cue could prevent illness and injury. It's also a great thing to teach puppies early on, to prevent stealing and attention seeking whilst you chase them around trying to get the post or your socks back.

About Resource Guarding

Resource guarding is a completely natural behaviour for dogs. Dogs that live in groups with well-developed social skills are rarely overt with their requests to keep a resource. In this picture, our little dog is telling everyone not to come near that biscuit in her mouth, simply by the position of her ears.

Lacy was a lovely, easy going, wonderfully cheerful dog that came to us after five years of hardship. Yet, she was always easy to live with and this ear position was as far as her resource guarding went. Interestingly, the other dogs read this ear position with ease, and they respected it, which is an example of perfect canine communication. Most dogs do this when they have a valued resource. It's also part of the social communication of wolves, as it turns out.

Dogs that live with other dogs who don't understand them or with people who haven't learned their intricate language will guard more overtly. Like any other communication, if it doesn't work, it will get louder and more obvious.

Think about a time you have asked for something, politely at first. But when the other person isn't listening, frustration may occur as your patience is tested, and you might get sharp or louder. If the thing you're requesting is important to you, then you may feel pretty tense and your own communication will undoubtedly become more overt. This is often why dogs go from Lacy's subtle ear position above, to growling and snapping when they want to keep a resource. If a dog learns that no-one listens early in their life, they will bypass the subtle signs and go straight to defensive, seemingly aggressive signs.

For many years, dogs have been punished for wanting to keep something they particularly like. Growling and guarding have been considered a deadly sin, particularly where children and safety are concerned. Poor quality trainers still stick their hand — or a weird glove on a stick — into the bowl of a hungry eating dog. Lots of people still say that we must be able to take anything from the dog and they should *submit* and give it up out of respect. Overpowering humans tower over dogs that are just trying to eat their food in peace, to show their warped version of *dominance* over the poor confused dog.

We expect a great deal from dogs, and one of our biggest expectations is that they put up with losing choices yet carry them out without protest. It's not fair to them.

Having something they like and wanting to keep it is perfectly natural. How many things do you have that you would like to keep? I suspect it's many, much more than your dog has. I certainly do. My husband knows never to take anything from my plate when I'm eating. He wouldn't dream of it and he knows that if he wants anything that I order from a menu, he must order a portion of his own. We laugh about it, yet it's a fundamental right that all of us have, to be able to eat undisturbed or keep something we value. If anyone stood over me when I ate, I would be likely to bite them myself. Wouldn't you?

Dogs should be allowed to eat their food and treats in peace. It's a fundamental right to be left alone when eating. Make sure your dog gets peace and quiet to eat, by managing the environment carefully and respecting his right not to fear loss of his food or chews until he has finished them.

Don't get me wrong, resource guarding isn't something that we should allow to escalate until it's dangerous. Some dogs naturally guard and sometimes it must be dealt with. Taking or forcing a valued resource away from a dog is counterproductive though and will only ever succeed in making them more tense around resources. Even if the force is heavy and the dog gets hurt — seeming to give in — they are just internalising their stress. The urge to guard isn't cured, it's just supressed because the dog is too scared to communicate how he feels.

The way we deal with the onset of resource guarding is not to stop the behaviour, but to stop the dog's perception of the reason for it. When something is scarce, dogs guard what they have more. If they have been hungry or particularly want something, they may guard it. Yet if there is plenty of everything they want, there really is no need. Teaching to swap is a fundamental skill that prevents the dog holding onto something they think is scarce. They know that there's plenty and they won't miss out by swapping. This leads to a dog that is far more relaxed about resources than he would be if we just grabbed what he has and left him with nothing.

For this mission, you will need a few things that your dog likes. The idea in the beginning is to swap something equal to or above the value of the item the dog already has in his possession. So only give free access to low or medium value things at this stage. This sets your dog up to succeed from the offset. It's a good idea to teach your dog to swap when you're playing together, as this is the easiest time to do it and the time your dog is most relaxed.

As you're playing with your dog and they are having fun with something, introduce something they really like and ask them to swap. Add a new cue word at the point you offer the alternative and if you have assessed your dog's preferred items correctly, he should spit out the toy he has and take the thing you offer instead.

If your dog goes tense, is reluctant or doesn't want to swap, you need to raise the value of the thing you're offering in return, until he's motivated enough to hand over the thing he has. You can practice this everywhere you go — but always as a game — until your dog will swap anything because he always gets the better deal.

Eventually, your dog will choose to swap on cue without you having to worry about what he's swapping for. Just remember to keep things fair to him, because if he keeps getting a rough deal when swapping things that he likes, he may become reluctant to give them up at all.

Mission Accomplished

This mission is completed when your dog swaps happily without tension, five times in a row. This is an ongoing mission really because it can be practiced through engaging play at any point. On walks, at home and during other coaching sessions.

Important note: If your dog is an established resource guarder and anyone at home is at risk from their behaviour, it's worth finding a local professional to help you. When we live with and love dogs, we tend to be somewhat emotionally blinded if they show a behaviour issue; I certainly do, so a second pair of trained eyes will always help. Remember to vet them carefully and ensure they are educated, positive and ethical in their approach. Feel free to email me if you need help finding someone. My details are at the end of the book.

Mission Ten. Relax

Our final mission is linked to impulse control which is particularly good for dogs who act before they think things through. Relaxing in a suitable space is a form of boundary learning which can be taught, resulting in a dog that is able to relax properly without thinking he needs to react to everything that happens in the home.

Every dog has the right to a warm, comfortable and safe space to relax and regenerate. Relaxation is a fundamental need for your dog, and re-balances his body and mind, from stress hormones and adrenaline built throughout the day. It also provides the right environment to deal with his experiences in the world and will keep him healthy and happy. Without the ability to relax, a dog may be stressed, not be able to heal from minor or major health issues or recover from anxiety.

About Impulse Control

Impulse control is a fascinating topic because it applies to humans as much as it applies to dogs. Everyone's impulse control is different and based on our individuality, including the tendency to act on impulse and the way that we react when we do.

If we were to act on every one of our impulses, we would probably eat everything bad for us, buy all sorts of useless things, get into lots of road rage incidents and generally say the first thing that comes into our minds. If a dog were to act on every impulse he has, he would be on high alert and highly animated. He would snatch treats, jump up, bark at everything and probably guard a lot of things, too.

Symptoms of lack of impulse control in dogs include:

- Snatching food.
- Jumping up.
- Barking at lots of things.
- Chasing cats.
- Dragging on the lead.
- Dragging through doors.
- Diving out of the car on walks.

The good news is that impulse control can be learned and taught. At its foundation, the ability to control impulses is created by achieving mind space. When we teach mind space, we do so by giving the dog pause in the environment, so he doesn't feel compelled to act on the first impulse he experiences.

Some dogs are more susceptible to lack of impulse control than others and in different areas. Dogs have things they prefer, just like people do and their impulses will depend on what they like or want most of all.

You can begin the foundations for this mission by teaching your dog to wait before taking a treat.

Just sit on a chair and pop a low to medium value treat on your knee. If your dog is a snatch-and-grab type, keep your hand close enough to take hold of the treat again before he grabs it. Then if he tries to take the food, take it back. Your dog will likely then look a little confused. He may sit or take a step back. When he's settled, pop the food back on your knee and ask your dog to wait. Do this for only a fraction of a second before you give permission to take the food by delivering your marker. If you leave it too long, your dog may take the treat anyway, which is counter-productive.

After practicing the above a few times, you can teach your dog that their reward comes directly from your hand when you offer the marker. You will need to be swift with this as he will be used to taking it from your knee. So, pop a low value food on your knee and have two or three small – medium to high value – food rewards in your hand. As your dog waits for the marker whilst leaving the food on your knee alone, get your hand ready so it interrupts his journey to the food on your knee. Then reward from your hand two or three times and allow him to take the food from your knee. Then it's just a case of alternating hand reward and knee reward randomly until your dog never touches the food on your knee — without first getting your permission.

The above exercise is a simple way to teach your dog to give pause before acting on an immediate impulse.

Consider the following ways to practice:

- By putting the food on the ground and rewarding from your hand;
- By asking your dog to wait before taking a toy during a game; or
- By asking your dog to pause on walks, when you let him off for a free run, with the use of a wait, marker, treat and their freedom.

The mission itself is similar. Yet conducive to rest and relaxation for your dog, in a managed way. It's important that we use this particular cue at the right time rather than just at any point in the day.

For example, my dogs relax early in the morning whilst I write, then I next expect them to relax after we have been for a walk and they have eaten. It's reasonable to expect them to relax then, because their needs have been met. I also ask them to relax in the evenings because I usually set a few problems for them to solve in their playroom three hours after their walk ended. After their mental stimulation, which usually takes about half an hour, I give them their final meal and reasonably expect relaxation. I'm lucky enough to spend all day with my dogs and can do this with no problems.

Many people work though, and dogs spend a lot of time alone. Boredom and loneliness may set in and when dogs get the chance for interaction, they will usually embrace it. To come home from a day's work and say a quick 'hi' to our dog then expect them to relax isn't fair. A walk, a play and perhaps even a coaching session later, and we could reasonably expect our friend to be ready for a rest. Physical and psychological energy needs to be used up for a dog to be truly happy. If your dog spends a lot of time alone, it may be worth considering an excellent canine day care or dog walker to help share your guardianship duties.

When your dog is healthily tired and has fulfilled the things he needs, such as toileting, walking, playing, engagement and interacting, you can begin to tackle this mission.

Start by deciding on your dog's boundary point. This can be anything at all. A blanket is easiest because it's moveable and can go on their bed, the sofa (if they use it) in the dog's crate if they have one, or even in the car for long journeys. Ensure your dog can lie fully on the blanket and be comfortable. Decide also on a suitable cue word for asking your dog to go to their blanket or bed.

For this exercise we return to targeting, though we approach it a little differently this time around. Here's how we do it:

1. Put the blanket on the ground in front of your dog and pop a food reward on it, so that he has to step onto the blanket to get the food.
2. As he fully steps onto the blanket, deliver your dog's

marker, food reward and cue. Practice this a few times unto your dog gets the idea that getting onto the blanket is an excellent choice.

3. When your dog is ready, stop putting the treat on the blanket and just wait. If your dog gets the idea, he will step onto the blanket for the marker. If he doesn't get it straight away, pretend to pop a treat down — to give him a reasonable clue. Practice this a few times.

4. Bring the cue forward in the usual way, practice until your dog is getting on the blanket when you ask and is released when you give the marker and reward.

5. Move the blanket around to ensure that your dog knows it's that that he's aiming for. Then practice in a few different places.

6. Then it's just a case of shaping a longer stay on the blanket before the marker is delivered. You can shape this by waiting for your dog to sit or lie down naturally as he tries to solicit the reward from you. Reward the change of position instantly, then withhold your marker in the same way to increase the time he waits on his blanket.

It's an excellent idea to leave your dog's blanket on his usual resting place throughout the day whilst you're at home together because you can capture his choice to go to his blanket and lie down naturally, with an occasional marker and reward. It will also teach your dog that the blanket is his usual resting place and not just something else he is learning and having fun with. When the two things become threaded in your dog's mind, which may take some time, your dog will have learned to relax on cue and in general, which will be excellent for his health and wellbeing.

This mission should not be rushed. Practice it regularly but always release your dog earlier rather than later because this prevents him moving off the blanket of his own accord. Work steadily over a couple of weeks or even longer if you need to. Remember the importance of well-laid foundations.

Mission Accomplished

Your final mission is accomplished when your dog will go to his blanket — placed in his usual resting spot — on cue and wait there for full ten minutes.

The Optional Release Cue

Some coaches like to teach a release cue to follow a cued choice. It's completely up to you if you want to do it. It offers consistency to the dog and structure to the learning experience. Throughout the book, we have released with the marker and reward as its most conducive to a simpler way of learning.

A release cue means that the dog learns to wait after a marker, and reward is given for a formal release. It's useful on walks when letting your dog off the lead, or when asking them to wait before getting out of the car. A release cue is also excellent for reinforcing impulse control.

Common release cues are 'off you go' or simply 'go' but you can choose anything that you prefer. Your dog doesn't mind. My first Labrador enjoyed the word 'bananas' so we used that.

To teach a release cue, you can alternate the number of markers and rewards you give. For example, whilst we have been giving one marker and reward so far, you can actually use as many as you like. The important thing to do is ensure your dog knows that another marker and reward is coming, so just wait it out after the first one. You can make this really obvious by delivering your first marker and treat and holding the second one in front of your dog's nose before you mark and deliver the second reward.

As you deliver the second reward, add in your release cue and move away from your dog, then play!

Practice with a varying amount of markers and rewards, and after a few repetitions your dog will start to recognise the release cue. Then you can use it as a cued choice to end any other cued choice that comes before it.

Takeaway Points

- It's much better to teach an alternative choice than just ask a dog to stop making an unhelpful one and leaving a gap in its place.
- If a habitual choice is replaced by another choice, the first one can become extinct. Extinction means that the choice, or the related behaviour, goes away.
- If there's a reminder of the extinct choice in the environment, and it's reinforced just once, it is likely to come back stronger than ever.
- Resource guarding usually occurs because the dog is scared of losing something valuable to them.
- We must never punish a resource guarding dog or force their resource away from them. They are not being naughty, they are just being a dog.
- Plentiful resources within a safe managed environment will relieve the dog's tension around the things he's worried about losing.
- Impulse control coaching gives a dog space in his own head, so that he can make more informed choices.
- All dogs need a safe space and ability to relax.
- We must provide physical and mental exercise before we can expect our dogs to relax.
- A release cue can be taught and used with every cued choice you teach to your dog.

Enrichment Through Scentwork for Highly Aroused Dogs

Introduction

Dogs that have lots of spare energy are telling us something very important, that we need to make some changes to their lifestyle to better meet their needs. Often these changes are small and have big, positive effects for the dog.

Arousal is a natural state in the right circumstances. Some dogs become over-aroused or frantic regularly though and that's not good for them, it's also quite difficult to manage. Frantic dogs are not making conscious choices to act in the way that they do, their behaviour is all that they can offer because it's how they feel.

We can make positive changes to the life of the frantic dog by doing something very simple indeed, introducing scentwork, along with calming coaching and gentle guidance. The beauty of this approach is that rather than try and bring the dog's behaviour under control by introducing obedience commands or restrictions, we can greatly enhance their lives and our own simply by teaching new skills. This applies regardless of age, breed and prior training.

The effect of scentwork based skills are amazing. The dog uses up physical energy without being walked for miles and becoming an athlete. They get to use their natural foraging instincts, using up all that spare mental energy and can truly relax afterwards. In addition, your bond will grow and together you will have lots of fun.

The missions in this book are designed to grow skill in stages. There are ten of them and by the end your dog will be searching areas like a professional, and you will be an established team. It's a great introduction to life enrichment, positive canine coaching and professional searching with a dog. All rolled into one smart little guide.

If you would like to, please document your progress through each mission with notes and pictures. To see your evidence and read your story would truly make my day, feel free to post your story on my Facebook page at www.facebook.com/sallyanddogs visit my website at sallygutteridge.com or email me at info@sallygutteridge.org. I respond to every message.

Note: I refer to dogs in the book as "him" purely for ease of reading, the advice applies to males and females in equal measure.

Part One: Understanding

If your dog is frantic, has lots of spare energy or reacts very quickly and with excess animation to any kind of stimulation, he is likely to be susceptible to over-arousal.

Any dog may go from relaxed to aroused if he thinks something is about to happen that he likes or dislikes. That's a perfectly normal response to the environment. The dogs that appear naughty, out of control or bad mannered are often just aroused more than is good for them and this shows in their everyday behaviour. Over-arousal on a regular basis is the main cause of a frantic dog.

A common mistake that people make when they live with a frantic dog is thinking that all these behaviours are within the dog's control, when they're not. They are a result of an internal state manifesting in the dog's external behaviour. In fact, all dog behaviour is a reflection of their internal state. A dog that looks relaxed is usually relaxed inside and the dog that is frantic on the outside is usually feeling frantic too.

For example, a dog that relaxes easily might be waiting for his morning walk, half snoozing in his bed, and he hears the coat cupboard open, so becomes excited and aroused. His behaviour will become animated and he may whine, dance around and wait for the lead to go on. This is all perfectly normal excitement and after his walk and perhaps a meal, this dog will probably go back to snoozing, resting away his exercise and full belly for at least a couple of hours. The dog who spends his everyday life in a general state of relaxation will become aroused at positive and negative events and relax afterwards.

Another scenario might be the dog that spends his life aroused and is always in a state of some arousal. This dog may be waiting for something to happen for all of his waking hours – and for some dogs most of their sleeping hours too. This can occur for a number of reasons, all of which we will discuss in this chapter.

The behaviour of this dog in the home will probably be quite different, he will be animated, maybe destructive, he may attention seek or perhaps even self-harm by chewing his paws or other areas of his body. If something does happen – like the coat cupboard opens – this dog becomes an unstoppable force of movement and probably noise, he may continuously jump up, scraping legs and arms. The guardian of this dog may start to dread walks because putting the lead on is only the first step to a chaotic and unpleasant half-hour.

Symptoms of over-arousal include:

- Barking and/or whining.
- Waiting for something to happen.
- Excessive alertness.
- Listening for sounds outside the home and reacting to them by barking or becoming excited.
- Seeking your attention by trying to play or bringing a toy all day long.
- Jumping up.
- Grabbing and nipping at your hands or clothes.
- Height seeking by climbing the people around him.
- Frantic behaviour on the lead and on walks.
- Excessive panting and sometimes drooling.

In some cases, a dog that becomes aroused may show aggression or fear related defensiveness. This will take the form of growling, barking or becoming outwardly aggressive. This book isn't written to address this type of behaviour. It is important that if the dog you're caring for does these things that you seek help. First visit the veterinarian to check for possible health problems then find a suitable expert in canine aggression that works within the realms of science and positive, dog friendly methods.

The dog that spends his life aroused will become hyper-aroused at small events and is usually out of control. The good news is that arousal can be managed and changed when we understand the dog's individual needs and tweak their current lifestyle to suit them better.

The Risks

Without this knowledge there is risk, particularly from professional dog trainers that are not well-educated, yet advise dog guardians regularly. Frantic dogs get the blame for their behaviour and are misread, punished or forced into fearful states.

An example of this is the method of leadership or 'alpha' that has been perpetuated by the media over recent years. The simplified idea that the dog needs to know who is boss and this will solve all behaviour issues is sinister and destructive. Dogs are individuals that learn through repetition, motivation and reward, the same methods that people learn from. Dogs also suffer devastating self-esteem crashes if punished, forced or scared. Even extended confusion can damage a dog's wellbeing and the relationship with his guardian. Any trainer that thinks dogs are acting like wolves, that all wolves try to gain leadership of their pack, or that punishment is a valid regular teaching tool, is confused about dog behaviour science. It stands to reason that letting them near a dog will cause the dog confusion too.

To confuse a dog that tends to become frantic will usually lead to more frantic behaviour. The only exception is when a dog is taken well beyond their ability to cope and emotionally shuts down. This is the worst thing we can do to a dog in the name of teaching, because it means they have given up trying, are scared, depressed and intimidated. Unfortunately, it does change the behaviour and the dog looks like he's being good. His body language will be slow, careful, tense and his ears pulled back, lips pulled back and he will probably be trying to look and move away from the human that's doing it to him, eventually freezing altogether.

The picture shows a paw lift, tail tuck, tense body, head dip, half-moon eyes that show the whites and facial tension along with tense lips. This dog is scared and unhappy.

Whilst it's good to know what a worried dog looks like, we won't be condoning or delivering any of that treatment in this book. We will be understanding and channelling the dog's frantic energy into a good, relaxing Mission which will change his behaviour from the inside out – not the outside in.

Our teaching will result in a dog that looks like this, relaxed and happy.

Defining Arousal

When we consider behaviour, we must ask what is going on inside the dog. A dog that behaves calmly and is contented usually feels the same way. A frantic dog is usually experiencing a reaction within his body, that leads to panic, fear or stress of some sort.

There are two types of stress that a dog may experience. The first is helpful and aids learning, this is termed **eustress**. Peak performance is achieved in a state of eustress, it's when the dog experiences just the right amount of environmental pressure to carry out an important task to the very best of their ability. Eustress is the reason a mom can lift a heavy car from her child after an accident or a fearful public speaker can carry out the most amazing presentation.

The second type of stress is experienced when the dog cannot cope with the environmental triggers and goes into a state of **distress**. It could be easy to believe that distress is shown by an obviously scared or unhappy dog but in many cases this isn't so. Distress is also shown by hyper-arousal and animation. The frantic dog could easily be living in a body that is continually exposing him to excessive stress hormones. He literally can't help his behaviour.

The stress system of the dog, and of the human are pretty much the same. We both react to stressors with a fight, flight or freeze reaction. For a dog the fight may be barking and trying to scare something away, flight might be hiding or trying to run away whilst freeze is linked to emotional shutdown or learned helplessness. Dogs may also fool around when stressed, so they jump up, mouth hands and act generally goofy, to try and dissipate the tension they are experiencing.

The physiological stress reaction is universal but when experienced regularly the stress hormones never really stop being produced, so the dog can never relax fully. As part of this the dog's other systems slow down. Digestion, immunity and general hormonal movement within the body is hindered in favour of enabling the body to deal with what it considers a direct threat.

To summarise; stress is terrible for the dog's overall health and wellbeing and doesn't always look like stress.

Why Dogs Get Frantic

We must never lose sight of the fact that dogs are individuals. What worries one may not bother another and not all highly aroused dogs are stressed, some may just be bored and need an outlet for their energy. Every dog that shows heightened arousal levels may do so for one, or many, of the following reasons.

Genetic Influence

The domestic dog comes in all shapes and sizes. Some are happy to snooze the day away and others need something to do every day that uses up their energy and enables them to rest properly and truly, deeply relax.

The broad range of canine needs and behaviours is – in part - based on the range of dog breeds and their individual genetic influence and personalities. Whilst this book is about helping the bouncy dog focus and truly relax, it's important that we discuss what drives his behaviour in the first place.

There have been many ideas presented on how dogs joined people at close quarters and stayed so integrally part of our homes and hearts. The common theme throughout the most recent theories is that they evolved into the tamest wolf type animals, because we had plenty of waste food. Early human settlements may have been attractive to the tamer of the wolf's ancestor, based on the leftovers that humans discarded, a habit that has evolved with us to the present day.

Whilst we inadvertently offered food to animals that were hungry, we naturally attracted the boldest and bravest of the bunch. They became regular visitors but at this point they were still breeding naturally and choosing their own partners for reproduction – in a process that we call **natural selection.**

Any species that has plentiful resources – food and safety – will reproduce more. More reproduction leads to a boost in the population of that species, in a process termed **relaxed selection**. It's simply a case of ingrained species survival to reproduce whilst safe and when there's plenty of food to create strong offspring.

Whilst all this was happening it's thought that the species may have split into two types of animal. The split is considered to have occurred because the braver animals were able to get close to people and the anxious ones were not. The flightier animals moved away and continued to live in the wild, hunting for their food and naturally becoming the Gray Wolf that we know today. The closest ancestor to the domestic dog – through DNA - is considered to be the Gray Wolf which maintains this as one of the stronger current theories.

As relaxed selection occurs, early dogs became braver and friendlier towards people. Studies show that a change in evolution can actually change the appearance of an animal too. Coat colour, ear shape and general appearance have all been shown to change when a wild animal becomes tamer.

The next stage in the evolution of the domestic dog was a big one. We realised we could benefit from dogs, they could assist us with tasks such as obtaining food and guarding possessions. We may even have befriended them at this point and simply treated them as companions. We started interfering in their reproduction and **artificial selection** began. Choosing the mother and father of a litter of puppies will have an effect on the puppies so we chose for the traits we wanted to enhance. For example, sighthounds for their speed and ability to catch prey, or scent hounds for tracking over distance.

That's a brief and potted history of how the domestic dog's ancestor became the many breeds of dog that are recognised today. It's relevant to every single dog because it means that working breeds have been finely tuned to work over thousands of years, so we can't expect them to live quietly in a home with no mental stimulation. If we do expect that from them, they may develop hyper-arousal type behaviours, obsessive behaviours and habits that we consider problematic.

In many cases we have created dog breeds that are prepared

for a busy lifestyle and role and then expected them to live quietly and peacefully in our homes without the mental exercise that they need. We can also fall into the trap of believing that long walks are enough for a dog or lots of retrieve games will tire them out. In many cases it will but if the mental energy is not used up then we are creating an athlete dog with excessive, untapped mental energy.

Physical fitness and unused mental energy is one of the most likely routes to hyper-arousal. A body and mind that are bursting with excess energy are not conducive to relaxation or true rest.

Lifestyle contributors to frantic behaviour may include a lot of physical exercise, triggers in the environment or fears and sensitivity to things in their life. Diet is also an important factor when we consider behaviour, particularly hyper-arousal.

Food

Over recent years the dog food industry is being increasingly questioned. Highly coloured, preserved and processed foods are being replaced by dog guardians with fresh and cooked meals. Dog food is a hugely profitable niche if the manufacturer can create a big cost divide between the creation and sale price of their product, unfortunately the worst foods are heavily marketed, and the biggest cost is to the health of our dogs.

Just as bad food causes physical, mental health and behaviour issues in people, so it does in dogs. An ideal food for any dog contains all the vitamins and minerals, the right amount of calcium and all ingredients are instantly recognisable by their name. Long chemical names, cheap fillers or hazy ingredients should ring alarm bells if found on even the most expensive foods. Dog food can be supplemented with fresh vegetables, meats, beans and pulses. Variety is the spice of life and this applies to the dog's diet as much as anything else.

Physical Exercise

Too much exercise can also contribute to over excitability. It's easy to fall into the trap of walking longer and longer plus throwing toys to ensure our dogs are well-exercised and happy. Sometimes though, it's better to do less physical exercise and more mental stimulation, to aid relaxation.

Excessive retrieve games and ball launchers can be counter-productive to relaxation. The dog that continually chases a ball is using only part of their natural inherited stalk, chase, catch/kill and then eat sequence. This is the sequence that their ancestors used, and the Gray Wolf still uses, as part of the carnivorous lifestyle. When used naturally, the chase and capture/kill is relatively brief and followed by a long time relaxing, chewing and eating. When we manipulate this sequence with a ball launcher, we interrupt it and the dog gets the adrenaline rush of the chase over and over – but with no effective final chew and relax. This is why ball launchers can exacerbate hyper-arousal.

Triggers

A dog can learn to be over-excited by triggers in his environment. A houseful of children for example is usually considered a lively household and a puppy growing up there may become a lively dog.

Lack of learning general manners and behaviour, along with a lack of guidance can lead to a stressed dog. For example, a Labrador puppy may be welcomed to jump up when he's tiny, so he believes that's a perfectly normal way to act, and it gets him attention.

If we don't teach the puppy otherwise, when he gets to 30kg he's still likely to be jumping up but may be no longer welcome as he's quite the bruiser by this point. Then his jumping up gets out of hand and the dog is blamed, leading to him trying harder and harder to please his people in the only way he knows how because it's worked before – jumping up.

This dog is now in the position that he doesn't know what to do to make everything OK and to make his human happy with him. He just keeps doing the same thing because it worked so well in the past, leading in many cases to blame and punishment because the human simply doesn't understand the dog's motives. Add the poor quality professional trainer that uses force and punishment to this scenario - the poor dog won't know if he's coming or going.

Luckily if we are prepared to put in the effort, we can gain plenty of knowledge of how dogs learn. We can therefore not only recognise why this dog is jumping up, but we can also motivate him to do something else instead. Via guidance and skilled coaching, we can follow a simple process of teaching a replacement behaviour and rewarding it enough that it becomes the dog's behaviour of choice.

The human understands their dog, the dog understands what is required and is motivated to change his current default behaviour to something that is less full-on. Everyone wins.

There are many, many more reasons for behaviour, the dog could be ill or in pain, having a reaction to medication, or scared. If a dog's behaviour changes suddenly, the dog should always be taken to the veterinarian to rule out sickness.

The Good News

The good news is that if I have just described your dog, there is an answer. You don't have to walk your friend for miles to tire them out. You can throw away the ball launcher, or at least put it in the back of the cupboard, because there is a perfect solution to naturally relaxing your dog – life enrichment through scentwork.

Engaging your dog's brain and nose gives them a task and purpose that easily surpasses the daily walk. If you are walking miles to tire your dog out, you can stop that and split the time between scentwork and physical exercise. Balance is the key to a relaxed dog and whether your friend is a bored companion breed or a highly aroused working breed, you can use their mental energy by introducing enrichment through search. As a wonderful side effect your relationship with your dog will be enhanced, you will become a true team and together you will have lots of fun, in short - everyone wins.

Takeaway Points

- A dog's behaviour is an external display of an internal state.
- All dogs are individuals and have individual reasons for their behaviour.
- Arousal is a normal experience usually triggered by something in the dog's environment.
- Hyperarousal is excessive arousal that makes the dog appear frantic.
- Hyperarousal is often associated with stress, but it can also be associated with lack of mental exercise, sometimes linked with too much physical exercise.
- There are a number of reasons for a dog to be frantic and every dog will be slightly different.
- Food, genetic influence, physical exercise and triggers can all cause arousal and hyper-arousal.

Part Two:
Settling and Learning

Hopefully by now you will have some idea of your dog(s) and the reason they are often so highly aroused. It might be breed type, it could be lifestyle and maybe you were doing something with best intention, but have realised it needs to change.

Arousal doesn't always mean that the dog is stressed and unhappy. It just means that they are fizzing with energy which shows in their behaviour. This could be nervous energy, or it could be excitement that's misplaced. The behaviour could be led by the stress response, or it could be learned and reinforced in the environment. By watching the dog carefully and noticing what excites them, what seems to trigger a frantic state, we can understand how the dog experiences the world. We can also begin to make subtle changes to the dog's life that will change overly busy behaviour into relaxation.

When a dog jumps up, mouths, bounces around and scrapes it can hurt. It's natural to respond by pushing them off, exclaiming the shock and pain of a scrape to a bare leg, or to greet with lots of love and chatter even though the dog is already over excited.

Settling down is paramount to positive change. If we greet our frantic dog with a high pitched voice and animated movements, we are reinforcing their own excitement. If we move slowly and quietly, we are leading the dog by example into a calmer state. If you watched your own interaction with a frantic dog, from the outside, could you honestly say that you settle or excite them with your behaviour? What about any children the dog has contact with, do they add to the arousal or calm the dog down?

Our aim in this book is to calm the dog down, for his sake and the sake of those closest to him. We can do this by using carefully delivered coaching of calm behaviours, using positive reinforcement, alongside brainwork through scent. Because we want to get going on lowering the dog's arousal quickly, we will begin introducing activities now, and use them alongside further learning throughout the book.

Mission One. Find the Food

It's part of our culture to walk the dog and provide him one or two meals a day. That's food and exercise – it's how we meet a dog's needs. Dogs need much more though, like us they need the right kind of physical exercise, proper mental stimulation, play, the chance to use their natural skills and the opportunity to practice natural behaviour. This is why when the busy natured dog has had a walk and meal, he's often still looking for something to do.

Food will always motivate a dog. Eating keeps him alive and even the fussiest dogs get hungry. When we think a dog is not motivated by food, it's usually because we haven't yet learned how to use the right kind of food, in the right way, for motivation.

- Scatter feeding is simple yet can use your dog's scenting ability enough that he properly relaxes afterwards. Simply find a food that your dog loves and scatter it around the home or garden, in tiny bits and at a reasonable portion and let him sniff out the food and eat it.
- Many dogs love scatter feeding so much that they will ignore the bowl with food in but eat every last scattered scrap, engaging their mind and body simultaneously. This type of engagement will use up lots of excess energy and the dog is highly likely to settle afterwards.
- If you suspect your dog isn't going to get immediately stuck in, start with less food in a smaller area. Make it extra special to sniff, for example grated cheese or tiny bits of chopped meat and build from there.

Important note; use scatter feeding before or as the dog's meal, rather than after their meal, as a full belly is not conducive to foraging. Remember also to avoid using too much extra food, or the dog will soon not be hungry and may even put on weight.

Mission Accomplished

This mission is accomplished when your dog can successfully spend fifteen minutes sniffing for food, happily and confidently.

Why Foraging is so Effective

As humans we like nothing better than a plate of tasty food in front of us, I grew up eating huge carbohydrate-based meals that stretched my young stomach way beyond its capacity time and again. This has resulted in disappointment of perfectly reasonable meal sizes for many years as an adult. Food is a pleasure, a social occurrence, both comforting and rewarding for us. We can easily project that to our dogs, gradually growing the size of that meal in their bowl, when in many cases they would really rather forage.

Foraging for food has been a main Mission for dogs for thousands of years. If we offer them their meals in a bowl all the time, even though they may love their food, we are creating a missed opportunity for them. Up to a third of their life pre-domestication would have been focussed on finding food, that's a third of 'empty time' if we don't allow them to continue using that skill.

Alongside the opportunity to find their food, foraging is an excellent opportunity for the dog to use his amazing nose. The dog's ability to detect scent puts our own to shame. Long ago we too would have been able to smell things like hidden food and even sickness in each other. However, our lives have become extremely comfortable and we don't use the sense of scenting like we used to so over generations it has faded.

Everything has a smell which is based on diffusion. Everything in the world is made up of tiny particles, including ourselves. When particles reach the edge of something, they diffuse into the air and it's that diffusion which carries scent. Scent diffuses differently from different things, so gas and vapour smell most, oil and liquid next and then solid articles diffuse with less scent as their particles are most tightly packed. The scent that we recognise is tiny particles entering the air around the object or item.

Most food types smell quite strong. Cheese, meats and kibble are some of the strongest smelling foods there are and perfect for sniff games. Be careful which kibble you choose though, as some dog foods are not particularly healthy. The other option is to choose cat kibble, which will be much smaller – check the ingredients in the same way though.

When a dog sniffs something smart happens. The particles enter the nasal cavity, then a split occurs. Scent and air take different routes, air carries on to the circulatory system providing the body with the oxygen it needs, whilst scent goes to the brain to be processed.

The dog then exhales the used air through the slits at the side of his nose rather than pushing the air back out directly through his nostrils which would also push out any incoming scent. This leaves the dog able to continually draw in scent through his nostrils and up towards the olfactory area of his brain, gathering information.

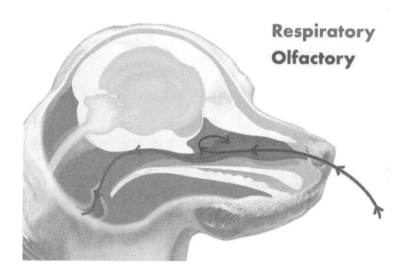

Respiratory
Olfactory

All this is happening whilst the dog forages which is why it is so relaxing and uses up so much energy.

The Scent Picture

Dogs 'see' in scent. We walk into a room and gather information predominantly through visual information. Dogs walk into a room and gather information through their nose.

So, if your dog goes into a room and realises someone has accidently dropped something tasty, they can go right to it because the scent is diffusing from the food and the dog just needs to follow the increasing strength of scent until he reaches his prize.

In the same way, if you're walking your dog at the park, off lead, and he catches a scent particle of nearby diffusing fox poo he will be able to follow the particles right to the poo and be shoulder down in it before you know it is even there.

Dogs don't only use scent to find the prize though, they use it to determine everything. To identify each other, to recognise us and to 'see' exactly what's going on in an area at any given time.

Mission Two. Calming through a Marker

The second mission is something you may already have done, we are going to introduce a marker for when we begin to use scenting as a task later and to help calm your frantic dog as soon as possible. A marker is something used in canine coaching and particularly positive reinforcement. This connection between sound and a reward has now become one of the most used tools of positive canine coaching.

A marker is something that tells your dog that they made the right choice. A natural marker is delivering a food reward, but dogs do multiple things very quickly and it's easy to miss the exact point that we want to reinforce, so a marker is used to pinpoint the choice. Using a marker makes timing easier, because it helps us to mark the exact choice we want to reinforce, with one single, known sound. The sound is paired in your dog's mind with his motivating reward. Then it has the ultimate power for reinforcing choices to change them from awkward ones to excellent ones.

The reward used with a marker will be small amounts of motivating food. Try to consider food reward on a scale of desirability. Number one might be dry food whilst number ten is smelly cheese. In between there may be healthy dog treats, fruit, peas or types of meat. Your dog will be highly motivated by the food higher up the scale and sufficiently motivated by the food lower down. You can use food higher up on the scale when your dog needs a real boost to learn. It's a good idea to start as low down the scale as works, because that gives you options when you need to offer something special. If you start at number ten, your dog will soon be used to that tasty food and become satiated, leaving you with far less options.

When we use food to teach anything new, such as searching, it's a natural reinforcing reward. The term reinforcement simply means that we make something stronger. When we reinforce a bridge, we add steels girders to it, to make it stronger. When we reinforce a behaviour, we add a rewarding event to it, to make it stronger in the same way. For the purpose of understanding, try to consider positive reinforcement in mathematical terms.

For example, if the dog offers a bark **(x1)** for some of your food and then you give them some of your meal, you are naturally adding strength to the act **(+1)** and the behaviour is likely to get stronger. The result that we see is a dog that barks more, because his personal steel girder in this situation is a bit of tasty food.

Food is essential for life, so it has special importance. The professional term for food in learning is primary reinforcer. We can create an association in the dog's mind with food, so when the dog hears the marker, he knows that food is coming, and he will naturally see the entire thing as associated with whatever he was doing at the time the marker was delivered.

Choosing a marker for a dog that tends to become over aroused is important, because a delivery of your marker will either settle or excite your dog. In fact, everything you do, from the tone of your voice to the movements of your body can be delivered in a way conducive to lowering arousal. So, monitor yourself carefully when interacting with your dog, are you moving in a way that helps him to stay calm and settled or are you delivering praise in a way that makes him far more animated?

All markers work so well because they are a mutual understanding of acknowledgement. You can use one marker or many. A traditional one is the clicker which makes a neutral sound to show the dog he has got something right. The clicker is a small box with a tiny plate of metal that clicks when pressed. If you press it without associating it with reward in the dog's mind, your marker won't work.

The marker is used to pinpoint the behaviour at its exact display point, and to let the dog know the specific behaviour which led to a reward.

The association between marker and reward must be carried out before the sound will have any effect. This is particularly important if you are not using a spoken marker. The first thing to do is decide which marker you would like to teach initially.

Teaching A New Marker

To associate the marker, choose a quiet area with no distraction. Along with a few handfuls of treats that your dog likes; they should be tiny, small enough to taste but not big enough to chew, as chewing can be distracting for the dog. If you have decided to use a clicker, have it to hand.

Then simply spend five minutes or so repeatedly delivering the marker and then giving the dog a small food reward. Your dog may be extremely over excited at this new game, particularly if he's generally aroused. Usually I would sit on the ground when teaching a marker but if your dog jumping on you because being on the same level gets him excited, perhaps sit on a chair or even stand up. Alternatively, if he jumps up when you're standing – sit on the floor and he may settle – it all depends on your own dog's personality and state of mind.

You can use this experience twofold for a frantic dog because after the first few deliveries he will be waiting for the marker anyway so time it well and deliver it during a pause in his movements and animation.

Dogs are smart. So, whilst you are teaching him that your marker means a treat, you can also be teaching him that the marker is most likely to be delivered when his movements give pause. It won't take long for his pauses to become more frequent and last longer.

An important thing to remember is that your dog will usually take all his behaviour from you. So even though you might feel excited that it's working, don't raise your own voice, get animated or outwardly over-enthusiastic in your success or your dog will get over excited too and that's counterproductive to our task. Keep calm, use gentle praise, slow movements and act as you want your dog to respond, calmly and with grace.

Repeat this little exercise for five to ten minutes for a total of five times over a couple of days to ensure your marker association is nice and strong. The further along the process you get, the calmer your dog should become, because when he gives pause a marker is delivered and he gets a reward.

The Food Grabber!

If you live with a food grabber, marker introduction can hurt. Small – or even large – eager teeth scraping repeatedly on the tender skin of your hand may put you off playing this game altogether. Here's a tip:

- Put a small bit of food in the palm of your hand and close your fist around it.
- Offer your closed fist to your dog and he is likely to try and get the food.
- Wait until he pauses and open your hand, so he can have the food.

Practice this little trick as few times and your dog will know that the key to getting the food is not to snatch, but to offer a pause and the food will magically appear.

Testing A Marker

At this point make a determined effort to have tiny food rewards to hand in the places you frequent most often. So, in the lounge at home where you sit, in the kitchen and anywhere else in the home that you and your dog share regularly. Pop a handful of tiny treats in a bowl in these areas, well out of the dog's reach because you will be using them.

During the day, when you're not in a coaching session you can test your marker, whilst reinforcing calm behaviour.

When your dog is calm or gives natural pause in his everyday life deliver your marker. If he turns or approaches expectantly you have made a successful and positive association with the marker – Great! Give your dog his treat and go back to what you were doing.

It might seem counter-productive to disturb a calm dog but remember that your dog will always associate delivery of the marker with the exact act he was carrying out at the time he heard it. So, he will always return to that act as it produced a reward. It's a good idea to make this part of your daily routine for the next couple of weeks. It only takes a moment and repeated a few times a day will teach your dog how rewarding calm behaviour can be.

Things to Avoid

Learning to time your delivery of your marker can be quite a difficult process, some people are totally natural and quick thinking, their timing leads to success very quickly. Other people have to work at it and get into all sorts of messes based on timing being a fraction of a second out of where the marker should have been delivered. Don't worry if you're one of the latter group - I am and have reinforced plenty of odd things in my dogs over the years. It does take practice to get the timing right, but our dogs are very forgiving and if you remember to keep things calm, in this instance you can't go too far wrong.

When you have introduced your marker, you must always associate it with a treat. Never deliver a click without following up with a treat and in the early days do the same thing with your marker word. If you deliver a marker regularly without giving the associated reward, your marker will lose its power and cease being a marker at all.

The other thing to remember is that the marker isn't a distractor or recall. If you use it to get a dog's attention whilst he's doing something undesirable, you are marking that undesirable act and your dog will remember and repeat it. This is particularly important with frantic dogs because we can be tempted to try and use it to initiate calm, in the heat of the moment, that's not how a marker works though. We must wait for a tiny bit of calm and mark that – otherwise we will be teaching the dog to be frantic for a reward.

Mission Accomplished

This mission is accomplished when your dog fully understands that a second marker will lead directly to a food reward. You can test this by delivering the marker when he's doing something completely unrelated (but desirable) and he responds to it.

Takeaway Points

- Foraging for food is a natural and relaxing behaviour.
- Scatter feeding will use up a lot of energy and aid relaxation because sniffing is tiring.
- Scatter feed your dog regularly with a food that motivates him to seek it out.
- Go at your own dog's pace so if he isn't interested just drop five bits of tasty food and build his confidence and ability from there.
- Marker use is an excellent positive coaching tool.
- For a frantic dog choose a neutral or calming marker, such as a clicker or a calmly delivered word.
- Make and maintain marker association by always delivering a treat, even if you marked the wrong thing otherwise the marker will lose its power.
- Utilise the times your dog naturally gives pause and mark and reward the quiet times.
- Never use the marker for distraction or recall as this will be counter-productive.
- Have confidence in yourself and your ability to help your dog. Like everything, marker delivery and timing needs to be learned so don't worry if you get it wrong. Frantic dogs move quickly. We all get it wrong sometimes, practice makes perfect and you have already succeeded by reading this book and making positive change.

Part Three:
Inspiring Confidence

Without knowledge and investigation, it could be easy to believe that an over-aroused dog is also a confident one. This is not always the case though and often the dogs that become frantic are also low in confidence. Their behaviour is a symptom of being unable to cope in the life that they're in. They don't trust others or don't feel capable of dealing with things – which then become their triggers – in their everyday environment.

Confidence and outlook are two things we can assess by observation.

Outlook is determined by whether the dog has a positive expectation of outcome in any given circumstance, or a negative one.

Some dogs have an overwhelming negative bias which shows in their behaviour. The negative bias is natural and learned. Humans and dogs all have a natural negative bias, it's what kept us safe during early evolution. The individuals that expected danger in every situation were cautious and careful so stayed alive long enough to reproduce and pass those cautions genes on, over and over again. The ones that didn't expect danger were in danger more often, therefore may have been killed or eaten and didn't live long enough to reproduce. We have evolved to be careful and so have our dogs.

That's not the end of the story though because from the moment a dog is born, he will be learning how much danger there is in his world. He can just as easily learn a positive bias which in most situations will overcome his biological default. With nurturing throughout development and by being ever successful in his endeavours, a puppy can learn that his actions will be successful at least most of the time, so he will have self-belief and an expectation of success.

For many dogs though, particularly the ones that have developed fear, stress or over-arousal in response to triggers, they are living within their own negative bias. Their biological program and their life so far has taught these dogs that a situation will lead to a negative result and the behaviours they show are based on that expectation. For example, the dog on a lead that barks defensively and bounces madly when he sees another dog is expecting a bad result if that dog gets any closer. The dog that has been taught with punishment expects to be punished.

The good news is that by confidence building through

scentwork based tasks, we can turn that negative bias around and show the dog how successful he can be. The dog's new outlook will start to shine through and his expectations will become positive, in all areas of his life.

Mission Three. Building Determination

By this point your dog should be happily and confidently finding and eating scattered food that you have dropped for him, he should be thoroughly enjoying the process.

You can tell he's enjoying the task by carefully watching his body language. A wagging tail, complete immersion in the task and loose body language all portray a happy dog. After he has found every scrap your dog should be able to relax and have at least a short rest. This process will be doing wonders for him, even at this early stage.

How quickly we introduce this third Mission depends on the confidence of your dog. Some dive straight in whilst others need some encouragement.

About Encouragement

We can encourage dogs to take part in the tasks we create for them by providing vocal confirmation of their efforts. For some dogs this works great, for others it does nothing or even worst puts them off. With all types of canine coaching it's a good idea to listen carefully to your own voice when working with your dog, and that's no less important when we are setting tasks to build determination.

We can be tempted to talk way too much to our dogs at all times, if we do this, the use of vocal encouragement becomes lost in the constant chatter. For example, if you use your voice as a marker, your dog could easily miss the sound if it's delivered in a stream of other sounds. Another thing we can be tempted to do is use a high pitched, excitable voice to dogs that are already highly aroused, this can easily cause over-excitement for them and exacerbate their tendency to become frantic.

It's a good idea to use few well-timed words rather than a flow of chatter. A well timed 'yes' or 'get it' for a dog that's losing confidence but trying – followed by a gentle hooray when the task is solved – is enough.

As all dogs are individuals, yours may love those words of encouragement, not care about them or could even find them distracting. Watch your dog and you will learn whether or how much to use vocal encouragement.

My own dogs are a mixed bunch with this type of tasking;

Chips gives up easily and needs some extra help and encouragement but is so happy when he achieves.

Vinny and Posy love the tasks set to them and work methodically through them getting the hidden morsels, utilising their paws and noses to the best of their ability –

needing no encouragement at all.

Holly, who was rescued from a puppy farm at six years old where I believe she was born, is another matter altogether. A small Yorkie, scared of everything but our home and immediate family, Holly is a tiny ball of determination when given a food finding task. She rips through thick cardboard likes it's tissue paper, jumps three times her height and generally works the room like a bull in a China shop.

You can find out your own dog's style of task solving by watching and testing him. You may be surprised. Some dogs seem extremely confident and bark at everything they see on walks, but set them a task that's a fraction too difficult and they give in. If this describes your own dog, you can be certain that the barking outside is based on poor self-belief. The dog that doesn't believe he can do the task often barks because he doesn't think he can deal with the stranger in the park so shouts as loud as he can 'keep your distance or else'.

For this task you will need some small, motivating and tasty foods and an old towel. The idea is to take the visual aspect away and get your dog's nose working on its own. Whilst building perseverance to work a bit harder for the food. It doesn't matter where you play this but it's better to keep distractions low and only play with one dog at a time.

Show your dog that you have food then go out of his sight with it. Don't give him the opportunity to follow you, close a door behind you or create another barrier so you are out of view.

Place the towel on the ground, put the food on it then fold it in half so the food isn't obvious. Next let your dog into the area and watch.

As he has been scenting for scattered food for a few days, and you showed him you have some food, he will start looking for it immediately. This is the point where his level of confidence will show. He will go straight to the towel and will do one of two things:

1. Sniff it, realise the food isn't there and move away.
2. Start moving the towel around to get to the food that he knows is there.

At this point, as with all canine coaching, you can adapt your own responses to the capability and confidence of your dog.

If he moves away, he may return to the towel and try again. If he does, vocal encouragement might be enough to get him digging for the food. The beauty of your dog knowing a marker at this point is that you can use it to encourage his efforts at solving the task. Each time he tries to move the towel, mark and drop another treat on it. Then wait until he tries to move the towel again and mark again. Continue this until your dog finds the food inside and you have started the growth of his confidence.

Your dog might just dive right in and solve the task in seconds, that's amazing. You can work up to more elaborate folds of the towel very quickly. Making the task harder will encourage more brain and nose work, resulting in more relaxation afterwards. Dogs all react differently to their food being in a towel. Their confidence and tenacity will dictate how difficult you should make the task.

No matter how your dog responds to this task, your role over the next few days is to make it challenging for him, but not so challenging that he gives up. Make your own input, whilst he's solving the task, encouraging but not distracting or too exciting. Get inventive, use more towels, fold them so the food is well hidden and generally build your dog's self-confidence and determination whilst using up chunks of that mental energy that is making him frantic.

Mission Accomplished

This mission is accomplished when your dog can confidently and happily find all the food in a towel that is folded in a way that takes reasonable sniffing effort.

Dogs That Won't Try

Hopefully by now you have a dog that is progressing in his capacity to try the new tasks you are setting him. Sadly though, some dogs just don't have the self-belief to attempt to solve even the simplest of tasks. This usually occurs with dogs that have previously fallen on hard times and severely lost self-confidence or have tried things in the past and learned that their efforts make no difference.

There's a term for dogs that have learned not to try, it's called learned helplessness and it's a behavioural term used for dogs and people. Based on a distressing experiment, which I won't describe here, learned helplessness is a form of choice depression specifically based on the ability to try new things.

When a puppy is born, they try all sorts of new things and if those things work the puppy will repeat them because he liked the result. With freedom and encouragement this is how the puppy learns. With positive coaching we can reward all the good choices and teach the puppy that they are worth repeating.

A dog that finds himself in a situation that he doesn't like and chooses to leave that situation usually learns to steer clear of that type of situation again. If he is in a painful or distressing scenario and doesn't get the chance to leave it, or an attempt to leave it results in the situation getting worse, the dog will stop trying and just accept his fate. He has learned that he is helpless in that situation and depending on their life experiences, some dogs learn that they are helpless in all situations so stop trying anything at all.

Holly, my tenacious little Yorkie arrived with us in a state of learned helplessness. Puppy farmers are renowned for being cruel and rough with the dogs they breed from and Holly had suffered at their hands for years. She had raised many litters in the dark and had them removed before doing the same thing all over again. She was terrified of people and just went stiff and waited for whatever was going to happen, to occur. This little dog had learned that she had no power over her life or body so stopped trying.

In the same way if a dog is not taught via kindness and guidance, they can learn that they are helpless. Force and fear-based training often doesn't teach the dog correct choices before it starts punishing the wrong ones. For example, rather than teaching a dog to walk on a loose lead the forceful trainer waits for the dog to pull, then checks with a painful collar around the dog's neck. In this scenario – whilst the word heel may have been used before the check – if the dog doesn't know what the word means because he's not been taught, they will do the most natural thing to them. In the case of a painful collar around their neck, the most natural thing to do for them is to try and get away.

Knocked for six by that check they will try harder to get away, then be checked again and again. Hurt, confused and probably in pain, this dog then gives up trying anything at all. This scenario or ones similar to it only need to be repeated once, before a dog loses all confidence in himself.

The good news is that learned helplessness can be reversed. Depending on its severity it may take a few sessions, or it could take much longer. We can certainly teach a dog they are not helpless, that they can do everything they try to do and that industriousness pays off, by changing their life in two ways:

1. Setting them tasks that they will succeed at.
2. Offering them choices that are carefully presented to ensure their success in making the right one.

Mission Four. Multiple Tasking

By the time your dog gets to the point where he can confidently find his food in a towel that's tied in a multitude of positions, the fun really starts. In the same way that we set-up his success with the scatter feeding and towel, we can present tasks that raise your dog's confidence in endless ways.

Your dog may have got to this point very quickly, or he may have taken longer. None of that matters though because by the time you are here, your dog's mental health and ability to relax is well on the way to improvement.

Next, we get really imaginative. Here's where we safely utilise all sorts of household items and even recycling, to present the dog with as many chances for success as possible. Tasks need to be achievable, safe and enjoyable.

Here are some ideas for easy tasks to create that your dog will enjoy:

- Prepare the towel as usual with food in but this time

put it into a cardboard box.

- Put food directly into a box and loosely put the lid on for your dog to get in.
- Wrap food in paper for ripping and place a few around the room.
- Put food at the bottom of a box and some of your dog's toys on top of them, so he has to remove or forage in the toys to get the treats.
- Pop food in each pocket of a muffin tray with a ball on top, so your dog has to move each ball to get each bit of food.
- Hide food at your dog's eye level around a room or garden so he really has to sniff it out.
- Tuck some food into a few cardboard rolls and close off each end. Hide the rolls around the room or garden for your dog to find and then open to get the food.
- Use packaging for tasking. For example, an old instant gravy pot with food in and a ball on top will provide a good challenge. An empty cereal box with food in and sealed will provide ripping fun or even the waste from parcels you have ordered can be set up to give your dog some foraging fun.

The list above is certainly not exhaustive. The only limits are your imagination, and all of them are totally free to create. A lot of the items above get thrown away or recycled anyway so why not recycle them through your dog first?

I suggest you spend a few days doing the first three activities, particularly if your dog is low in confidence. The more tasks he achieves at, the more confident he will be for the next step in your journey together.

Mission Accomplished

This mission is accomplished when your dog has solved ten different problem-based tasks to get the food reward within them.

Takeaway Points

- All dogs are different, and their self-confidence varies as much as people's.
- Some dogs have learned that making choices isn't possible for them, so they stop trying.
- We can help all dogs learn to make successful choices and build their self-confidence by providing them with achievable tasks.
- Some dogs need more encouragement that others, by watching a dog we can see how much help he needs to succeed in a task.
- Beware of talking too much or in an over excited voice as that can be distracting to a dog, or even make him over aroused.
- Marker use is an excellent way to reinforce the dog's effort and show him that he's doing the right thing when trying to solve a problem.
- When the dog has the idea, withdraw the marker and allow him to work it out.
- Tasks can be created from all manner of household items and recycling. Dogs love ripping to get to food that they have sniffed out.
- Get imaginative and have lots of fun along the way.

Part Four:
Starting to Seek

After a couple of weeks problem solving and working as a team, your dog's confidence should be nice and high. He should be relaxed and able to rest better, because he has regularly used his mind and nose. In addition, his general state of mind should be improved. If you have continued to mark and reinforce his peaceful behaviours, whilst maintaining your own, your dog should also be less frantic and easier to live with.

I suggest that you don't cease all the steps we have covered so far. They should be an integral part of your dog's life, and your life together from this point on. Even if you get hooked with searching, still give your dog problems to solve a couple of times a week because they will enrich and improve his life, plus of course they will keep him calm.

Now we can begin to teach the basics of searching for a specific scent. This is where the real fun begins.

The first thing to do is decide what scent you would like your dog to learn to find. Choosing a scent must be done with care because of the dog's tender nose. There's no point asking your dog to find something that's uncomfortable for him to sniff or that's particularly difficult to find. An excellent scent is ginger. This is because you can break a small amount of ginger biscuit and hide it in your dog's search item. Then when he finds it, he can eat it, providing your dog with extra motivation to seek and find the prize. A healthy and smelly dog treat is another choice but be sure it's not used in other areas of your dog's life, otherwise it will confuse him.

Good scents include:

- Vanilla
- Ginger
- Catnip
- Sage
- Aniseed

Scents to avoid are:

- Chilli
- Pepper
- Citrus or citrus oil
- Perfume items
- Rosemary or Lavender.
- Toxic substances.

We avoid the scents because they are too strong and may be

uncomfortable for the dog to work with.

The keep things simple, I'm going to use a ginger biscuit throughout, but the choice of scent is yours. The important thing to remember is that the same scent should be used from this point on. So, the dog knows exactly what he's 'looking for'.

Next you need to decide what the scent will be in, the dog's specific search item. A search item is necessary because if we asked our dogs to search purely for ginger biscuit, they will eat them as quick as they find them, resulting in a plump dog high on sugar. We also teach search through a particular set of lessons, one of them is an effective retrieve and if you can teach your dog to retrieve a ginger biscuit then give it back, you are a better coach than me.

When we choose a search item, we must consider the following points:

- Scent particles will pass through soft materials quicker than solid ones. So, a wrapped and knotted cloth with a bit of ginger biscuit in will smell much stronger than a sealed plastic box.
- The item must be comfortable for the dog to hold, carry and play with in his mouth, because we will be doing all these things as part of the lessons.
- The item must be safe and cause no danger to the dog. So be sure that the dog can't swallow it, that bits won't

fall off or can't be chewed and eaten.

- Ideally the item should hold the prize, let the scent out easily and not be opened too easily or the dog will still get to eat the biscuit far more often than he should.

It's also a good idea to consider your dog's natural confidence here because the smellier a search item is, the more easily the dog will sniff it – which is a great confidence boost. In addition, the easier an item is to open, the more likely the confident dog is to get more biscuit than is good for him.

A small Tupperware box with holes in to let the scent out, put into a knotted sock is a perfect search item. The holes let the scent into the sock, which holds onto the particles and creates a scent pool in the area. It's also comfortable for the dog to hold.

The term scent pool describes the density of the scent itself as it diffuses away from the item. So as the item sits in an environment with no wind and little air movement, scent will diffuse around it in an even way, the same way in all directions. This is known as a scent pool.

If there is air movement in one direction, the particles get caught up in that movement and generally make a cone shape as the move with the air. It's when the dog's nose detects the scent particles that he realises the item is close and follows the pool or cone shape of scent density, right to the source – his prize.

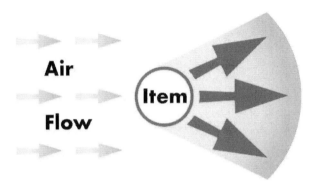

Here's how scent passes through or around items in the area based on their density. It generally passes around hard articles and obstacles.

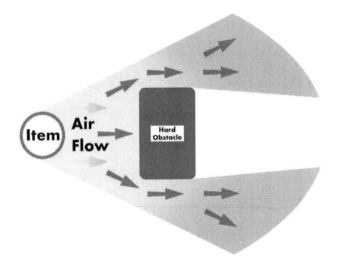

More scent will pass through soft obstacles, resulting in a different scent picture for the dog.

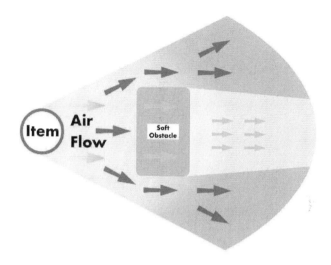

If the obstacle is big, like a wall or a building, the scent will usually bounce off it and back into the area, producing a turmoil of scent particles with high density.

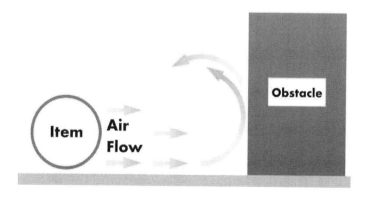

Up until this point your dog has been building self-confidence, industriousness and (hopefully) quiet determination through solving problems to get food. Now we begin searching for a scent, where instead of him getting the reward from the find, he gets it directly from you.

To prevent confusion, we carry out this new learning in bite sized chunks, to ensure the dog knows exactly what to do.

Mission Five. Targeting

By this point your dog should be familiar with the use of a marker when he's getting something right. We are going to use that marker throughout the next few activities. We are also going to introduce the cue word for searching.

Cue Word

A cue word is a prelude to an act or choice you would like your dog to make so if we use the word now, we establish it nice and early. This can be simple, **find** or **seek** is perfect.

Targeting is fun and another aspect of positive coaching that can be transferred to many different activities. When we see dogs that dance with their people on TV or at dog shows, targeting has been an integral part of their learning. To target a dog to something means that they learn to touch it with their nose or paw via positive reinforcement and usually, the use of a marker.

Targeting your dog to an item is a prelude to teaching him to retrieve a specific item, in this case his ginger prize. We will then make the retrieve so complicated that it merges into search naturally and easily for your dog.

Start the session with your treats, marker and your prepared search item. Sit on the ground with your dog if he's calm enough for you to do that, if not sit on a chair or stand up. By this point he should hopefully be calm enough to share a floorspace with you.

Then you can target your dog to his search item by following the steps below:

1. Pop the item on the ground in front of your dog and wait a second. He might touch it immediately, which is great, if he does – mark and reward the touch with a treat. Otherwise you can help him by popping a tiny treat on the item.
2. When your dog gets the treat and inadvertently touches the item, mark and give him another treat. Do this a few times and then progress to just pretending to put a treat onto the item, but still click as the dog touches it.
3. Next you can include a cue word as the dog touches the item. Then move the item around and click as the dog follows it and touches it.
4. Continue to move the item around into lots of different places and heights, then as your dog touches it, mark and reward. The stronger this behaviour is now, the better foundations to his ability to search will be laid for later.

We initially introduce the cue word as the dog makes the right choice, this is to begin the association with the behaviour, nice and early. Then we can bring the cue forward as the behaviour is learned, until the dog can offer it on cue, because he understands exactly what that cue means. The steps below break this down nicely:

Step one: Introduce the cue.

| CHOICE | + | CAPTURE WITH MARKER | + | CUE | = | REWARD |

Step two: Link the cue to the choice.

| CHOICE | + | CUE | + | CAPTURE WITH MARKER | = | REWARD |

Step three: Give the cue for the dog to make the associated choice.

| CUE | + | CHOICE | + | CAPTURE WITH MARKER | = | REWARD |

Mission Accomplished

Mission five is accomplished when your dog can successfully go and touch the item for a marker and reward and has repeated the process in fifteen different places, varying from nose height to ground level.

Throughout reinforcement-based learning there are three ways you can teach your dog something new. The one you use will depend on your dog and how much help he needs. Each of them are best taught with a marker for accuracy and mutual understanding. They are described below:

Lure

The easiest option for the dog is to lure him and mark the desired position or choice with your marker. It's easiest because it means we show the dog exactly what we want from him by having him follow a treat into the position. This technique is good for dogs that have low confidence because it sets them up to succeed with guidance. An example of luring in this situation would be to have the dog follow a treat in your hand to the search item and as he touches the item whilst taking the treat you will mark the behaviour. Marking the position in this instance is also capturing it.

Capture

To capture a choice or position means that we deliver a marker at the exact moment the dog makes the required choice. This is something you have already being doing since you began introducing the marker. Marking any choice or act is essentially capturing it, reinforcing it and making it stronger.

Shaping

Shaping means that we capture a number of behaviours that lead to a desired end result. We will be shaping a search and find over the next few steps by creating a chain of less complication choices, until your dog can carry out quite a complicated search. Shaping can be carried out with a mixture of luring and capturing, depending on the dog's needs and confidence at the time.

Recognising Confusion

Confusion throughout coaching should be avoided if at all possible. The steps of teaching something new should be delivered in a way that keeps the dog's confidence high and confusion low. It does happen though and even the best canine coaches can end up with a confused dog at some point in their teaching.

Recognising that a dog is confused is vitally important to productive learning. If we don't recognise confusion early, it can become stress. Signs include:

- Trying to move away.
- Scratching furiously.
- Picking up toys.
- Sniffing the ground.
- Trying to distract with play.

If your dog does any of these things or acts strangely

otherwise, he may be getting confused and you could be asking too much from him too soon. Take a step back to relieve his tension, because if you don't, learning won't occur, plus he will become stressed.

Stress when it develops from confusion can be shown in the following ways:

- Yawning.
- Lip and nose licking.
- Fooling around.
- Panting.
- A furrowed brow.

If this occurs it's important to alleviate the tension quickly by changing the subject, setting an easy task then rewarding it to build the dog's confidence.

Play

Play is exceptionally powerful to learning. Not only does it make the dog feel good, but it also cements memories from the lesson that preluded the game.

Within the dog's brain there are a number of neurotransmitters that affect how he feels. One of them is Dopamine which is linked with motivation and memory. If we play with our dogs Dopamine floods the brain, making them more motivated and quickly establishing a successful memory of something that without play would take much longer to create.

Mission Six. Target to Retrieve

After your dog is confident to touch the item with his nose, start to withhold the marker. Do this carefully because if you move on too soon, your dog will lose confidence and will be less capable of learning.

The idea is to withhold the marker, shaping the behaviour of picking up the item. With the dogs that find this difficult, a simple shaping session would focus on clicking the open mouth, the mouth around the toy and lots of small attempts at lifting it.

This may take a few sessions depending on how confident your dog is. Some dogs can bypass this stage altogether. The trick here is to get the click in before the dog ends the behaviour, the click will usually and naturally end the behaviour, but that's fine. A retrieve may come easy for some dogs but for others you may need to build it up by rewarding the tiniest foundation of the act then building his confidence and capability.

You can grow and strengthen the retrieve in the following ways:

1. Hold the dog, throw the toy and send him to fetch it, this can increase in difficulty as the dog learns and he will also be starting to use his nose to locate the toy.
2. Play fetch and throw a few times so he gets and extra reward of play, whilst he's still learning to retrieve.

3. When your dog retrieves successfully, start to throw the toy out of sight, into complicated areas, to encourage him to use his nose more in finding his prize.

Remember to always use your cue for finding the item when your dog is chasing it. That's a great habit to perfect now, because it will come in handy later.

Easy Blueprint to Retrieve

Here's a quick recap on targeting to the scented search item, through to retrieving an item that your dog can't actually see. The following steps can be adapted depending on your dog. Your dog might flow through them all or even miss some out because he is finding it easy You may get stuck on some because your dog is finding it hard. If you get stuck on something, simply make things easier by going back to a step that the dog finds easy and rebuilding from the earlier level.

1. Place the item on the ground and put a tiny treat on it.
2. When the dog takes the treat, click and reward from your hand too. Repeat this a few times.
3. Pretend to put the treat on the toy and click as the dog touches it. Practice.
4. When you get to the point where the dog will touch, click, reward repeatedly start to move the toy around in the local area, always keep the toy on the ground at this point and remember not to make it too difficult in

the beginning. Practice.

5. Add the cue word for search, that you have decided on and say it every time the dog touches the toy. The process should be, touch/cue and mark. The idea is that the dog links the three things in his mind with the idea that he will get a reward.

6. Start to put the toy at different heights in the area and repeat step 5. Practice this.

7. By this point the dog may be picking up the toy or may still be touching it. The main aim is that he goes to it and touches it.

8. Shape the behaviour of picking the toy up if you need to because your dog doesn't do it naturally.

9. Shape a simple retrieve and use the same cue word you have been using for search.

10. Gradually introduce complicated retrieves and out of sight retrieves by holding the dog, throwing the item out of sight and releasing him to sniff it out. Keep using your cue and practice until the retrieve is strong and flawless.

Mission Accomplished

Mission six is accomplished when your dog has successfully retrieved the item from ten different places within your usual coaching area.

Complex Retrieves

Here's some ideas for complicated retrieves, don't do too much too soon though. Remember to set your dog up to succeed and raise the complexity, only when he's ready. These tips are not exhaustive, so feel free to get imaginative:

- Hold your dog by his collar or harness then throw the item away and turning the dog around so he doesn't see it land. Then let him go to sniff it out.
- Holding your dog then throwing the item out of sight. There are many ways you can vary this. The item can be thrown into roughage or out of sight around a corner or into a box.
- Varying the height that the retrievable item is thrown to will strengthen the dog's resilience to fetch it too. So, hold the dog again throw the item into bush or similar raised area. This teaches the dog that his prize may not always be on the ground.
- Throwing the item into areas that the dog has to work at, to get out. Be sure not to put the dog in any danger though, no gorse bushes.
- Get imaginative when building the dog up to difficult retrieves. Make it fun, play, have an excitable assistant if possible – to help with the throwing - but never overwhelm the dog. Cater everything to the individual dog's ability and confidence.
- Use your search cue throughout, every little bit of learning helps.

Mission Seven. Generalisation

Generalisation is sometimes called proofing and it simply means that we teach a dog to respond to cues in a multitude of situations, before we can be sure the behaviour is fully learned.

Lack of sufficient generalisation can result in a dog who knows a cue perfectly at home but loses all ability to understand it when he's at the park or elsewhere. When your dog learns something new in one environment, for example at home with no distractions, we can't expect him to know the cue in a place where there are lots of distractions.

Think of it this way, you may make coffee in your machine every morning at home, with automatic grace. When you go on holiday, everything is different in the new kitchen. You have to find the cups, learn how to use a new machine or cafetière, and turn a different way to find your sugar and milk supplies. In essence you have to learn to make coffee all over again.

Imagine if on that first day someone was stood next to you demanding that their coffee is supplied right now. They may be saying "come on you know how to make coffee" and getting frustrated with you, making you feel terrible. You might get confused, you may be a bit stressed and because you haven't practiced this behaviour in this place before, you can't think straight enough to do anything at all.

After a few days practice though, it all comes naturally to you and you have learned the task in a new situation. Your coffee making procedure is generalised, which is exactly what happens when we take our dog's newly learned behaviour into different situations.

Excellent generalising techniques re-teach the choice in new situations. It's important to avoid adding two difficult tasks together because this will cause confusion and upset the dog's confidence. When we raise difficulty, we also raise motivation. This makes sure the Dopamine is triggered and gives the dog a learning boost.

To generalise the act of targeting to your search item start in the house, move to the garden, then take it to the park or on walks. After the initial burst of walk energy is over and your dog is settled, whip it out of your bag and do a couple of minutes targeting at different heights, play with the search item and do some retrieves, then put it away and get on with your walk.

It's a great idea to pretend to throw the item then sneak it back into your bag, your dog will still believe it's in the area and that leaves him wanting more. This little addition to your walks is great fun and your dog will love it. It will also ensure you make his walks more interesting, that you could do something interesting at any time and that you're worth keeping an eye on.

General generalisation (proofing) will include introduction of everything your dog will see in life, along with adding strength to their new cue or choice.

Mission Accomplished

This mission is accomplished when your dog has successfully retrieved his search item in five different areas. The areas should include indoors, outdoors, in his usual walk area with no distractions, with reasonable distractions and on a high distraction walk. The things that distract your dog will be reasonably unique to him so keep that in mind.

Search Item Care

When transporting your search item, it's a good idea to remember that humans smell very strongly, and your dog could easily learn to search for your scent as opposed to his corner of ginger biscuit. People shed hundreds of tiny skin cells every hour and those cells smell like us. If we touch the search item or place we are putting it, we are contaminating the area and item with our own scent. Therefore, it's a good idea to keep your item contained either in a bigger Tupperware or plastic bag when transporting it, then just drop it onto the ground or hide it through the plastic rather than touching it. This will serve to keep the scent near the item and will also prevent it smelling too much like you.

It's also a good idea to clean the item regularly and certainly change the biscuit at least once every few days. To keep a fresh scent. Remember that the soap you use to clean it will have a scent too, so you may want to simply hand wash the sock and box in water before adding a fresh biscuit.

Takeaway Points

- Problem solving is an important life enrichment for dogs and should become a regular part of your dog's care and activity.
- Dogs can become confused when learning and we should look for the signs.
- Confusion can become stress if we don't change the situation.
- We can change the situation by asking for something simple instead then playing.
- Play increases the neurotransmitter Dopamine which enhances motivation and memories.
- Play is rocket fuel for learning and all canine coaching should involve lots of play.
- We can teach new choices by using a lure, capture or shaping. We can adopt one method or a mixture of all three.
- A cue is a word that the dog associates with a specific choice and all choices have different cue words.
- We introduce an early cue to associate it with the right choice in the dog's mind. Then gradually bring it forward until the cue preludes the dog's choice and eventually the dog knows that that specific cue is linked with the associated choice.
- Generalisation is the act of re-teaching a choice in all areas with all distractions until the dog can make the right choice no matter where he is.

- Generalising will be taught gradually at the dog's pace, with careful introduction of new areas and distractions. When we raise a distraction, we should also raise motivation for the dog as this makes the best choice the easiest one for him to make.

Part Five:
Your Search Dog Extraordinaire

When you have worked through the missions in this book successfully, your life with your dog will have changed. By this point he should not only be more settled but should have learned a solid foundation of scent related choices that have readied him for the next step.

If you have worked through quickly or are reading this for the first time with the aim of going back and following the steps on a practical level, great. I promise you that if you spend three sessions on each of the seven missions we have covered so far, your dog and your relationship will be calmer and easier.

Soon we will work on changing retrieve to search but first let's throw in one more calming mission for you - A quiet place.

Mission Eight. A Quiet Place

I toyed with the idea of adding this mission in earlier but

decided against it as I believe it's important that your dog gained confidence by trying new things, early in the process. However, if your dog tends to lack the ability to control his impulses, barks or jumps up and you're reading this book through first, feel free to teach this cued behaviour earlier. Just do it after you have started scatter feeding and foraging because your dog will be naturally calmer after those.

If you're teaching this as mission eight, the introduction of a quiet place is perfect, because your dog's confidence should be nice and high. Over the last few weeks your dog should have learned that he can succeed, that choices are rewarding and should have also been using up bags of energy which previously will have caused problems – because he didn't know where to put it before now. That's a great time to introduce cued relaxation.

A quiet place simply means that your dog learns to settle down in a place and practice controlling his impulses, which should be far more easily controlled than they were a few weeks ago. You may have heard the term impulse control before. It basically means the ability to take a measured approach to a current choice rather than just diving in and doing the first thing that comes to mind.

In my case, impulse control is least effective with food. I like to eat as much as possible, whenever possible. So, without taking a little mind space I find that halfway down a bag of chips is a common place to be. My own motivation for impulse control is clothes that fit and a healthy body/mind. You too will have impulses, they will be unique to your personality and life experiences. You may get angry when driving by someone that cuts you up, because you have been in a crash before, so you might swear and shake your fist if you give into that impulse. You might like sugar and getting stressed for some reason leads to an impulse to grab a donut.

In the majority we have learned to control our impulses to a socially acceptable level. Our dogs have a different experience of life to us though. They essentially live with aliens in a sometimes scary world. Dogs are also totally natural, they act as they feel at that moment and sometimes they have an impulse to do something awkward for us but perfectly natural for them.

Teaching your dog to settle in a quiet place will show him what you want, will aid him to relax and create some space in his mind, enabling him to realise there's a different choice to unabashedly giving in to the first impulse he experiences.

For this mission you need to decide on a new and unique cue word, a second word which you will use to release and a suitable quiet place. For example, you could introduce a specific blanket for settling on, which is portable, so you can take it anywhere. You can use you cue word 'rest' and to release your dog you could use 'off you go'. Your cues should be the ones that naturally fit your impression of the situation because they will be the easiest to use.

This task really isn't too different to targeting in the beginning. Instead of reinforcing your dog's nose touching an item you will be reinforcing his whole body being on the blanket. You can do this by using the following steps:

1. Put the blanket on the ground in front of your dog.
2. Drop a tiny treat on the blanket so that your dog has to step onto it to get the treat, mark the position and provide a second reward. Repeat this a few times. Add the cue word at this early stage and use it when your dog gets onto the blanket, to benefit from the early association.
3. Feign the act of placing a treat on the blanket and mark then reward directly from your hand. Practice a few times.
4. Move the blanket around the house and repeat steps one and two. Practice.
5. Soon your dog will be getting onto the blanket and looking to you for a mark and reward, that's great. Start to bring your cue word forward and instead of rewarding him from your hand, start to throw the marker reward a couple of metres away and as your dog leaves the blanket to fetch it – add your release cue.
6. After release and when he's fetched the nearby reward, your dog will look to you for the next step. If you wait quietly he is likely by this stage to get back onto the blanket – great! Deliver your cue as he steps onto the blanket, then mark and reward again in the same way.

When your dog is going to the blanket on cue, lengthen the time he stays there. You can do this more easily if you start the act of time increase by putting the blanket in a comfortable spot such as his own bed or a place on your sofa (if he's allowed there). The act of gradually increasing the time will naturally encourage the dog to settle down, but this stage needs to be practiced over a few sessions.

To rush here will likely result in your dog moving before his release cue and that's a new habit that is tough to break. With this in mind, try to always release a fraction early. Once the dog has chosen once to break from his quiet place, all on his own, he has learned that he can, and this becomes rewarding enough to repeat. It's much easier to release your dog early than for him to release himself. The key here is not to expect too much too soon, which sets your dog up for success and teaches big behaviours in small achievable chunks.

It's better to practice the quiet place cue after an activity, walk or after a meal and when your dog has toileted. Don't expect him to settle when he's full of energy. Remember everything we do with our dogs should aim to set them up for success and a satisfied dog is much more likely to settle down than one that's fizzing with energy.

Mission Accomplished

This mission is accomplished when your dog will go onto his quiet zone and settle naturally for a full fifteen minutes. This is the only mission that you do not need to complete before moving to the next one, as it can be practiced alongside continuing to learn search dog skills.

Mission Nine. Multiple Drops

Mission nine should be carried out only when your dog can fetch his item from the most complicated places during a game of retrieve. Being able to sniff out, fetch and play with his prize is highly motivating and an excellent foundation to begin more complicated search.

Now we can start to stretch his scent recognition a bit further. You can do this on your own by safely tying your dog in a place where he can see you (preferably on a harness to prevent pulling in anticipation as that will hurt his throat) or you can enlist the help of someone else. The idea here is to provide your dog with a few options of where his prize may be, so that he can really start to use his nose for finding the scent.

Here's how to do it:

1. Choose an area where there is somewhere for your dog to stand and watch, with a few different hiding places that he can see. The idea is that he uses his nose to get to the correct one.
2. Have your dog tied or held in the area so he can see all the possible hiding places and show him the prize – your search item.
3. Move away from your dog and tuck the prize out of his

sight then pretend to place it in four hiding places, but only drop it in one of them and return to your dog to show him your empty hands. Keep everything smooth at this point, so don't double back, just do one basic loop, like the image below.

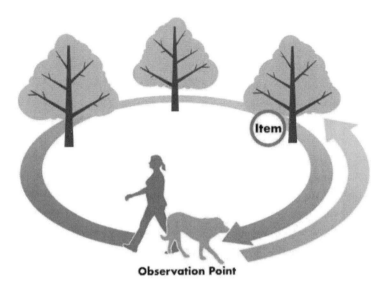

Observation Point

Release your dog, delivering the cue to find and then watch them. I can almost guarantee that your dog will go to the last place you visited first. If he doesn't find the prize there he will go to your second last hiding place and so on. How long he looks for depends on his sniff ability and confidence.

If his confidence drops, make the task easier by leaving the prize in the first place he's likely to visit and build to the following. If your dog's confidence is high you can shake things up a bit by touching all areas you visit and adding your scent to them, plus leaving the prize somewhere a little more complicated.

When your dog gets his prize it's time to celebrate. Use the power of play to have a really good game, do a couple of retrieves, a game of tug and trigger that Dopamine for his memory.

Mission Accomplished

Mission nine is accomplished when your dog can search five different possible drop off points and find his prize, even after you have touched all areas and hidden the prize almost out of sight – in five different search areas.

Include in your areas; an indoor room, your garden, a woodland with trees, a fence line with posts and an area with concrete floor with suitable hiding places – somewhere like a garage or car park.

The Art of Just Enough

When teaching something new it's important not to ask your dog to repeat the same successful lesson more times than holds their interest, or they will get bored and probably confused. This is particularly important for dogs that learn quickly, after one or two tries at something.

Imagine you had learned to solve one specific crossword. The first time you did it, the challenge is enjoyable, but now you know all the answers, have identified the words and where to put them. Yet I ask you to do it another five times, sitting in the same seat in the same room. You would soon get bored and frustrated by my odd requests, the words and clues would no longer challenge you and you would probably resent me a little bit.

Our dogs don't really do resentment, as to err is human, the dogs that get the idea quickly will want to leave though and the ones that lack confidence will get confused and self-doubt. Either way they will show similar behaviours, they may start displacement acts such as licking or sniffing. Your dog could look like they are ignoring you, which is their way of changing the subject, or they might show signs of stress such as licking lips or yawning.

Get to know your dog's *just enough* learning point and don't push him beyond that or your teaching will become counter-productive. For example, if your dog does an excellent find from a complicated multiple drop in a new area that's great! Don't repeat that exact scenario. Introduce a new area, find a new hiding place or take a new direction around the hiding places, or even better – celebrate with a game and call it a day for that session.

Mission Ten. Searching

When mission nine is completed your dog is ready to move on. It's a good idea to have a helper at this point if you can, for the first few sessions anyway. If you don't have an assistant you can tie your dog in place as you did on mission nine and do the assistant role yourself.

All previous missions completed successfully will ensure that your dog can move onto searching with ease. By this point he should know the cue for finding his prize and be pretty sure that his prize will be out there in the place where his cue is given. Then it's just a case of starting short and building up.

It's a good idea to return to a place where the dog has already succeeded in a multiple drop when you begin this next step. Instead of your dog standing in the middle of the hiding places as we did in mission nine, plan to have them facing the hiding places in a line going from closest to furthest away. The fence line practice area, with four or five posts or trees is perfect for this.

For this mission we start to get the dog's prize hidden before he enters the area. As we are moving on from big clues to actual searching on cue, this is probably the most important part of this mission to get right. Early hiding places should be obvious, they can get more complicated later, but for now we need to build your dog's confidence on this early step. The scent should be accessible and easily detected.

Consider the wind direction and any obstacles in the area. Ideally there should be little wind, so the dog can stumble into the scent pool or there should be a side wind across the hiding place, into the search area, so that your dog will enter the scent cone as he travels along the fence line. The first hide must also be only a few metres from the dog. Don't have the item hidden twenty metres away as the less confident dog may give up –

remember it's the first time we have ever planted the prize without a big visual hint, so initially we need an easy hide.

1. This step will ideally be carried out by your assistant. Have your dog static and watching the assistant walk along the fence line towards him, then the assistant will briefly show their empty hands to the dog. There is no need to pretend to hide anything here, the item should already be in place. This will be exactly as they would have done at the end of mission nine. The dog's mind then from memory, when released, will go straight into searching for the item.

2. Release the dog and give the cue for finding his prize. As the fence line is a natural boundary your dog should run up it and go straight to his nearby hidden prize, grab it and bring it back. Then you should both play to cement the experience.

3. Congratulations! You have now trained a dog that can search an area on cue and find a hidden scent.

4. Next it's a case of building one part of each search at a time. Increase the distance before the find, on some searches. Keep the distance short on some but make the hide more complicated by putting something on top of the item or introducing wind that takes the scent away from the hide and the search direction. Don't be tempted to make all parts of a search more complicated at once as your dog might become confused and lose self-belief. This final mission will be ongoing even after

it's accomplished – because search areas and hide opportunities are endless, even when your dog is a seasoned searcher you can find ways to challenge their new skill.

No Chatter

Whilst we have covered talking earlier in the process let's recap. When your dog is searching he will be working hard to negotiate the area and detect the scent of his prize. If you chatter whilst he's doing this you will either be distracting him or teaching him to ignore your voice, just as we ignore a radio playing in the background.

There are only three specific times you should use your voice during a search:

1. To give the cue at the beginning or if your dog gives pause because he's been distracted from the task.
2. To question and encourage him when his behaviour changes because he has recognised the scent and is near the hide.
3. To reward with praise and a game when he finds his prize and brings it back to you.

Excessive chattering is like micro-managing your dog and will always be counter-productive. No-one likes to be micro-managed, least of all the dog who is using his learning to complete a task.

Scent Recognition

Your dog will have a specific body language change when he detects his prize via its scent. You will learn to recognise his find language early in this mission. That's when you deliver your question and ask him what he has found. A question will spur the less than confident dog on to self-belief and the confident dog will also receive confirmation that he's doing the right thing.

When a dog gets a hint of the odour that he is searching for, he will often close his mouth. This gives him the opportunity to get more air up into the nasal cavity. This is one of the first signs of scent recognition and can be extremely brief but as you learn your own dog's habits, you may see this time and again, with the awareness of exactly what it means.

Your dog may be seeking the item but not be in the scent pool or cone, then suddenly he stops. He may do a check pace and turn his nose around to point it back to where he was when the scent hit. This is an obvious indication that the dog has scented the item.

If your dog loses the scent again he may continue in the direction he was heading. If he has hit a scent cone or pool, he will work through the scent with his nose, to detect the hidden item. As he does this your dog's body language will be more excitable, his tail will speed up and he will generally show more purposeful movement.

As we know scent travels. When an item is in an area and if it's warm, the scent particles get bigger and will rise, they may even be detected above the dog's head. Nose in the air and obvious scenting is an indication that the dog has caught a scent and is trying to work with the particles and get closer to the item. If the weather is cold scent particles get smaller and stay close to the ground, so your dog may detect his scent lower down on cold days.

Because we teach our dogs to search for their toy and a reward, they get excited when they find its scent. This is brilliant because a motivated dog enjoys himself and finds searching easier. The body language of scent detection is genuine excitement. Your dog might seem to go onto his toes, become busier and move more quickly. When you have seen it a few times you are more likely to recognise the change in your dog's behaviour than if you're seeing it for the first time. As your searching grows, so will your ability to read your dog's body language when he finds his prize.

Later on, when hides get more complicated, if your dog shows interest in an area they are likely to have found the hidden prize. They may refuse to move away from a specific point and attempt to dig or mouth at the area.

As all dogs are different, so will be their scent recognition body language. Some may be a mixture of any of the above and other dogs may show something completely original that tells us they *see* the scent picture. The trick is to know your dog well enough to notice any changes and use that knowledge to encourage them.

Hides

The hide is the place that the dog's search item is sitting, waiting to be found. They are split into six general types which can be swapped around for variety:

1. An easy hide is a place where the dog will detect the scent easily. For example, dropped into long grass or tucked behind a fence post. The easy hide is used early in the learning process to build confidence. It can also be used as a boost for the competent searcher, to give them a boost.

2. A difficult hide is where the scent will be more difficult to detect. For example, in a box with only a small scent escape path, at the dog's nose level on a warm day or on a windy day in a place where the direction of wind takes the scent cone out of the search area.

3. A known hide is where you know the location of the search item. This will help you to learn your dog's language early on and question at the right time. It also prevents confusing feedback to your dog when you misread his signals and question at the wrong time.

4. An unknown hide where someone else places the search item in the area. This is good for later on, well after you have proofed this final mission. The unknown hide is best practiced when your dog is

competent, and you have the confidence to read his scent detection signals. With this hide type, you are both being tested as a team. This is my favourite bit and is extremely fun and rewarding for both of you.

5. A fresh hide is a new hiding place where the item has just gone into the area and scent is still moving around. The fresh hide will have more than the scent of the item, there will be disturbance scent and scent from the person who set the hide, plus a scent footprint track to the place, all of which help the dog.

6. A settled hide is older than 24 hours and other scents in the area will have settled too. This gives the dog an accurate scent of their prize minus the disturbance of the fresh hide. Take care where hides are hidden because some wildlife love ginger biscuits and it's best to avoid sending your dog off on a fruitless mission.

Mission Accomplished

Your final mission is not the end of your journey, in fact it's just the beginning. To complete it though, you need to carry out five different short searches.

1. A minimum five-minute search with an easy, fresh hide, where your dog successfully finds the prize and brings it back for a game.

2. A minimum five-minute successful search and find with an unknown easy hide.

3. A minimum ten-minute successful search and find

with an unknown, easy, fresh hide.

4. A minimum five-minute successful search and find with an unknown, easy, settled hide.

5. A minimum ten-minute successful search with an unknown, complicated, settled hide.

Remember that every search should end with a reward and play as it will fuel your dog's learning, confidence and ability more than anything else you can offer.

Takeaway Points

- When your dog is using up their physical and mental energy you can teach him to retire to a quiet place and relax. To do this when the dog is bursting with energy is unfair and likely to fail.
- The quiet place provides excellent energetic balance.
- Remember to use the *art of just enough* when teaching new things.
- Practicing multiple drops in many ways and places will provide an excellent foundation to search.
- When we make one task more difficult we must make the others easier to grow the dog's confidence and competence.
- Your dog's behaviour will change when he detects the scent of his prize, the exact change will be unique to him.
- Don't chatter or micro manage your dog as this will distract him.
- Mix and match hides, difficulties, search length and areas in bite sized chunks and one at a time until your dog can search like a pro.
- Celebrate your new skill!

Summary

Thank you for coming on this journey with your dog. I hope you have enjoyed every moment and that your lives are enriched by the missions and your achievements. I also hope you have learned a lot along the way about how your dog thinks, learns and the motivations behind his behaviour.

I hope your dog has learned to relax through scentwork and that your relationship is greatly improved by the vast amount of new skills you have together. My ultimate aim for this book was to raise your understanding of your dog, settle your friend down and ensure that you both have lots of fun along the way.

Please visit my Facebook writing profile here https://www.facebook.com/sallyanddogs/ and I would love to see the feedback as you work through each mission. Pictures would be an added bonus and of course, any questions are more than welcome.

Thank you!

Final Note

Please could you leave a review?

Reviews dictate readers, readers mean better understood dogs and happier guardians. They also get this work seen by as many people as possible, so I would really appreciate it if you took a moment to share your experience. Thank you.

If you have any questions or just want to say hello, you can contact me at my website sallygutteridge.com or info@sallygutteridge.com. I respond to every single message.

Thank you for joining me.

Printed in Great Britain
by Amazon